"As a veterinarian, I view the stories in this book as vivid descriptio[...] picking up on individual needs of her patients. Over and over the a[...] relationship between animals and humans can lead to profound therapeutic, physical, and psy[...] healing. Your heart will be touched by the wonderfully told true stories of a pet therapy dog named Maggie, whose bedside interventions brought joy and healing to an entire hospital. From the pediatric floor, the terminally ill, and even the hospital staff, no one could resist the charm of this furry healer."

Dr. Paul Rennekamp
St. Francis Pet Hospital

"This book was a joy to read. It made me smile, laugh, and cry—all things that a good book has the power to do. As the administrator of a continuing care retirement community, I have the privilege of witnessing the powerful impact that these "visits" have on our residents. My hope is that this book inspires others to follow in this very rewarding work. To the Janets and the Maggies of this world, I will be eternally grateful."

Karyn Fleetwood, HFA, MSM, BSN, RN
Lutheran Community Home, CEO

"A sweet, sweet story of a dog's life in service to others. The author touches our heart as she conveys the love for her dog and weaves it into her role as a nurse. You will learn how unconditional love can heal spirits and ease our journey through life."

Vicki Johnson, RN, BSN, MSN, BC-NE
Chief Nursing Officer, Schneck Medical Center

"The book was so great! I loved it. I had moments with tears and moments with laughter. I thought I'd read half, go to sleep, and finish the next night. But I read and read and just could not stop until I finished it. The book reveals a new, soul-touching side of lessons learned from the dogs. The author's dedication will inspire others to pursue their dreams. It made me appreciate what Janet does even more now. And of course, it immediately made me think of some new tricks we should teach Bentley to show off to his patients."

Julie Case, Master K9 Trainer
Director of Training, K9 Camp

"A dog in church? In the sanctuary during worship? Why not? It works! I have a graduate degree in theology and have been serving in churches for years. But I cannot recall a time when I captured the hearts of children as much as one fluffy dog named Maggie did with one brief visit to our church. Kids put their guard down and really made a connection with Maggie. And she taught them essential truths in ways I never could. What a gift one visit can be!"

Pastor Aaron Rosenau
Faith Lutheran Church
Appleton, Wisconsin

THE VISIT

Healing Moments in Pet Therapy

Janet Myers, RN

Foreword by Anita Kelso Edson
Senior Director Media & Communications, American Society for the Prevention of Cruelty to Animals

AuthorHouse™
1663 Liberty Drive
Bloomington, IN 47403
www.authorhouse.com
Phone: 1-800-839-8640

Learn more about THE VISIT:
www.thevisitbook.com

This book is a work of non-fiction based upon the work and experiences of the author, Janet Myers. The names and images included in this work are used with the express permission of the persons featured within. Certain names have been changed or altered based upon the desires of the participants, or due to lack of express permission. Those names are modified to protect the privacy of individuals who do not wish for their names to be made public. The author wishes to thank all participants and supporters of this work, whether named or not, for without them this work would have been impossible.

© Janet Myers, RN. All rights reserved.

No part of this book may be reproduced, stored in a retrieval system,
or transmitted by any means without the written permission of the author.

First published by AuthorHouse 8-17-2011

ISBN: 978-1-4634-1810-6 (sc)

Library of Congress Control Number: 2011909785

Printed in the United States of America

Any people depicted in stock imagery provided by Thinkstock are models,
and such images are being used for illustrative purposes only.
Certain stock imagery © Thinkstock.

This book is printed on acid-free paper.

Because of the dynamic nature of the Internet, any web addresses or links contained in this book may have changed since publication and may no longer be valid. The views expressed in this work are solely those of the author and do not necessarily reflect the views of the publisher, and the publisher hereby disclaims any responsibility for them.

Scripture verses are taken from The Living Bible, copyright © 1971. Used by permission of Tyndale House Publishers, Inc. Wheaton, Illinois 60189. All rights reserved.

Front cover photograph: Marshall Memories

Back cover photograph: Peekaboo Photography

Chapter Nine images: Stephen Brooks Photography

CONTENTS

Photo List	vii	Expanding Our Scope	57
Foreword	ix	Embracing The Elderly	67
Preface	xi	Lost Vision, Gained Insight	73
Acknowledgements	xv	My Defender	79
The Ah-Hah Moment	1	**Succession Planning**	83
A Bit Of Convincing	7	**Her Final Curtain Call**	87
One Paw In The Door	13	**Transitions**	95
Getting Right To Work	19	**Starting Over**	99
Spreading The Word	27	**Very Big Paws**	105
When You're With Me	33	**The "How-To" Chapter**	111
Playtime In Pediatrics	39	Endnotes	117
Last Act Of Love	47	Afterword	123
A Spiritual Connection	53	About The Author	125

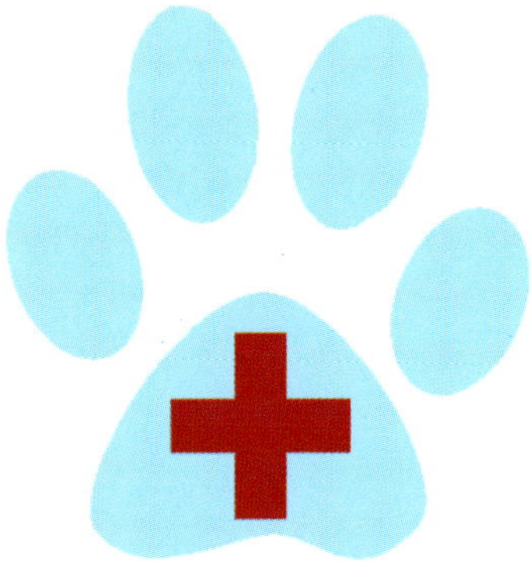

PHOTO LIST

1.1 Stowie

2.1 Ready for pet therapy
2.2 Preparing for certification

3.1 Waiting at the door

4.1 Trotting in to visit patients
4.2 Get well message from Maggie
4.3 Exhausted after visiting
4.4 Maggie and Mary

5.1 Getting to know the physicians
5.2 Second grade students meet Maggie
5.3 A big squeeze for the camera
5.4 Hangin' out in the Intensive Care Unit

6.1 Cuddling

7.1 Pet therapy dog in disguise
7.2 My personal childhood experience with pet therapy
7.3 Mikayla and Maggie—all smiles
7.4 Emma and Maggie share hugs
7.5 Joey and Maggie visit face to face
7.6 Maggie's Halloween costume entertains Peter

8.1 Together Mary and her father stroked the dog

9.1 A captive audience
9.2 Our children's message at church

10.1 Making reading fun in Miss Angie's class
10.2 Connecting with all ages
10.3 Maggie offers her paw
10.4 Well-deserved staff pet therapy
10.5 Maggie at the Employee Christmas party

11.1 Visiting with an elderly patient
11.2 An in-depth conversation without words

12.1 Good listening ears

13.1 Mutual understanding

14.1 Kandie
14.2 Kandie offers a hug

15.1 Portrait of Maggie

16.1 Fond memories
16.2 Bentley at five weeks

17.1 Dedication of Maggie's memorial
17.2 A compassionate face at eight weeks
17.3 Julie teaching Bentley to punt a football
17.4 Verifying patient identification

18.1 Bentley's learned response to "Are you shy?"
18.2 Dylan and Bentley—instant buddies
18.3 Bentley positions himself to visit

19.1 An engaging interaction

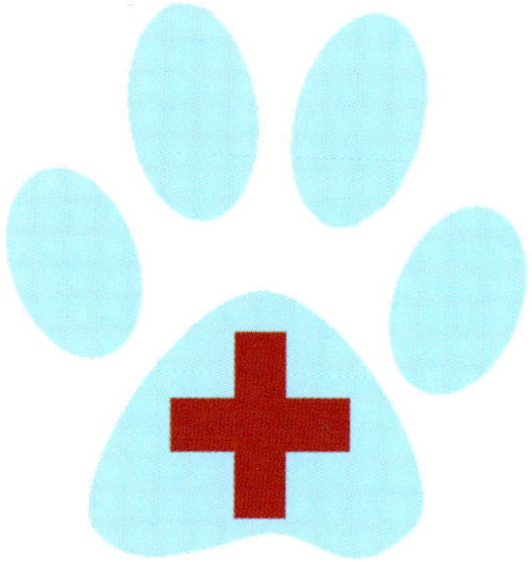

FOREWORD

When Janet Myers asked me to write the Foreword for this book, memories of my own experiences as an animal-assisted activities and pet therapy volunteer suddenly came back into focus. I recalled with fondness and clarity the many visits that I and my pet partner—a rescued Dalmatian named Scooter—made to schools, nursing homes, and hospitals both in Dallas, Texas, and later in New York City.

There is nothing like a furry, four-legged friend to prompt a reaction from even the most emotionally or socially isolated human being. Scooter's and my roster of clients included the lucid and lively, as well as those whose once-sharp minds had been robbed by Alzheimer's and dementia.

Aside from Scooter's "eye candy" appeal, he was sweet tempered and an ambassador, like Janet's Maggie and Bentley, for the beneficial effects of pet therapy (as well as proof that purebred dogs can be found in animal shelters). Countless books, articles, and studies tout the "healing power" of pets—how they have been shown to lower blood pressure, cholesterol and anxiety, increase self-esteem, stimulate socialization, and provide a host of other positive effects. Whether it's something as simple as a bedside visit or a goal-directed exercise where the animal has a defined role in a treatment process, there's no denying that such positive interactions with animals are a boost to human health.

There are many wonderful organizations that strive to promote the health benefits of animal-human interactions with the assistance of activity and therapy animals. Janet and her dog Maggie (and now Janet and Bentley) are the perfect example of a team that is making the most of the pet-health connection. Even if you are not part of a pet therapy team, you will be inspired and moved by Janet's story.

Anita Kelso Edson
Senior Director, Media & Communications
ASPCA®*

*Note: The opinions of Ms. Edson are offered in her personal capacity and do not necessarily reflect those of the ASPCA.

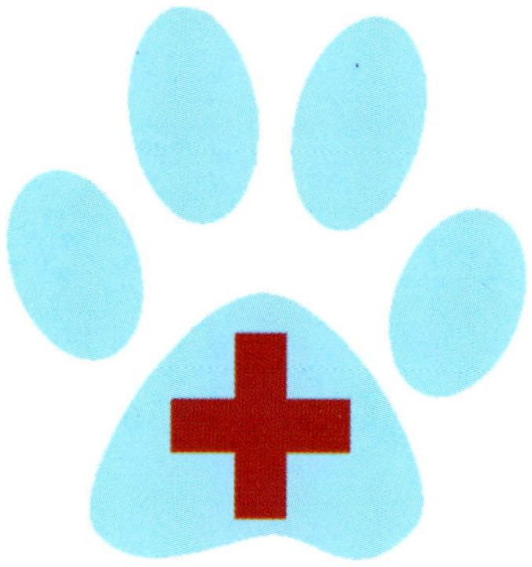

PREFACE

When my first Bernese Mountain Dog came into my life, I had no idea that she would become my beloved partner in pet therapy. I'd always been a dog lover, but my professional life as a nurse did not have any overlap with my personal life. In 2002, my world was forever changed. That was the year I began to explore pet therapy.

The writing of this book is the result of many years of personal experiences and research. As a nurse I cared for patients during the day, and as a therapy dog handler I witnessed the positive change in the persona of those same patients when I visited them with my therapy dog. That observation wasn't a one-time discovery. It happened patient after patient. As I shared my thoughts on pet therapy with my peers and was asked to give community presentations on the subject, I started investigating the newest studies on the array of phenomenal results that can occur with pet therapy. As I learned more about the data that supported my mission, my work as part of a pet therapy team with my dog Maggie grew naturally into an unofficial extension of my nursing career. It became in many cases the most rewarding type of bedside patient care I had administered in my thirty years of nursing.

My pet therapy journey has been enhanced with a deep understanding of why my fur-coated friends impact my patients' world. As a result, the gratifying encounters included in this book are accompanied by some fascinating data supporting the value of pet therapy in various patient types.

My hope is that these pet therapy excerpts, taken from my personal journey, will educate and inspire others. I invite those of you who share my passion for animals to experience the joys I have felt as you travel with my therapy dogs and me to the bedside of patients. I encourage you to explore your companion's natural abilities, travel the same or a similar worthwhile path with your pet, and allow your pet to serve others in ways that animals can so instinctively do. To aid you on your journey, this book includes a "how-to" chapter covering a variety of information to guide handlers and health care organizations.

This book is also meant for those dedicated health care providers whose compassion for their patients drives them to consider pet therapy as an adjunct to their care. As your patients' advocate, I urge you to consider the multitude of ways pet therapy can enhance your patients' well being.

As a nurse of many years, most importantly, I hope this book reaches families who have loved ones with health care needs. The physiological, psychological, and social benefits that occur with pet therapy are endless. This collection of true encounters describes how pet therapy can help in the healing process.

The foundation for this successful genre of care is the unparalleled connection between dogs and humans. These four-legged therapists, each unique, are truly gifted with the ability to administer care to patients in a broad spectrum of settings. The therapeutic nature of their interactions with humans offers a non-traditional, complimentary approach to patient care with outcomes that have been proven time and again.

What differentiates my unique style of pet therapy from others who are involved in pet therapy in one way or another is the combination of my health care experience and understanding of patient needs with some advanced dog training techniques at the bedside. The outcomes are both therapeutic and enjoyable for the patients, and the effects have been observed and validated by several different individuals, each with differing perspectives. Through the eyes of the patients, the observed reactions from the family members, and the clinical assessments made by the health care providers, the shared conclusion is one of amazement and healing.

A frequent thought I experienced when driving home from patient visits was wishing others could have accompanied my four-legged pet therapy partner and me. Then they also could be witness to THE VISIT and those simple yet powerful HEALING MOMENTS!

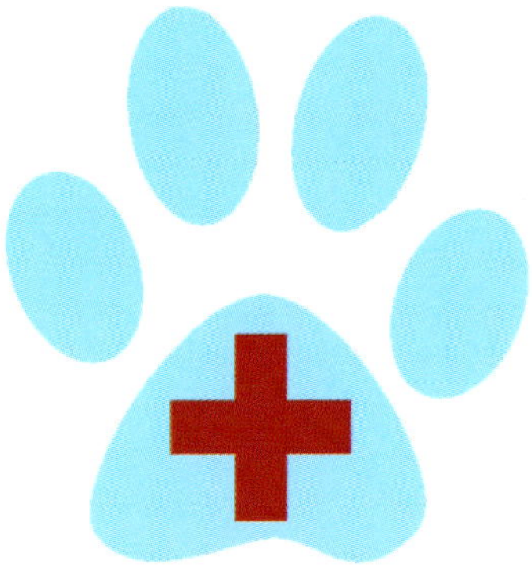

ACKNOWLEDGEMENTS

An army of individuals helped make this book possible.

I give thanks to God for orchestrating this entire adventure. I thank my husband, Gary, and my children, Andrea and Adam, for understanding my mission and absence from home for all of those time-intensive patient visits. I acknowledge breeders Lilian and Karen for placing these great tempered creatures in my care. I'm grateful for the open-minded and forward-thinking hospital administration and staff in support of pet therapy, and for all the patients and families who welcomed us into their world.

I thank my editor, Karen Roberts, for her meticulous work. And I thank the respected authorities who reviewed this book and gave valued professional testimonials. Specifically I thank Mrs. Karyn Fleetwood, Mrs. Vicki Johnson, Ms. Julie Case, Dr. Paul Rennekamp, and Pastor Aaron Rosenau. Thanks to my friend, Suzie McDonald, and my daughter, Andrea, and husband, Gary who were the first to review my manuscript and offer feedback as well. I am grateful for two talented photographers, Mrs. Jamie Marshall for her mulitple images of Bentley in his element, and Ms. Angie Gillaspy, for her lovely portrait work of Maggie.

I am most appreciative of Anita Kelso Edson, Senior Director of Media & Communications for ASPCA (American Society for Prevention of Cruelty to Animals). My sincere thanks to her for writing the Foreword of this book. I am grateful for her valuable reflection and keen insight of this personal collection of healing moments in pet therapy. May the value of this therapy, supported by research, become evident in the future homes of your ASPCA animals. I am hoping that the natural abilities of your rescued creatures are recognized and put to use in the vast world of human healing.

Most of all, I thank my two beautiful, furry partners that I have had the privilege of accompanying and observing for their endless display of unconditional love and unexplainable understanding of patient needs.

Stowie

1
THE AH-HAH MOMENT

Ten years ago I was barely familiar with the term *pet therapy*. Now it is my passion and an integral part of my contribution to and involvement in patient care.

I have been a part of the health care industry my entire professional career. Thirty plus years in nursing have given me the opportunity to care for a full range of patient populations, from the prematurely born infant weighing in at 1 ½ pounds to the elderly, frail, and often demented patient. As I would work with my patients, I not only felt responsible for their medical needs, but I also always tried to improve the quality of their day. My inner challenge was to carry on conversations with them that would result in at least a smile and at best a fun-loving discussion.

The hospital setting, although necessary, can often be lonely, mundane, and sad. It is especially so for those patients whose stay is lengthy and whose prognosis is grim. To lift the spirits of my patients, I would find myself telling them stories about my pets. Those simple yet personal stories usually started with, "So, are you an animal lover?" Rarely did I come across a patient who didn't welcome a warm, fuzzy tale of one of my pets. These sagas would typically lead to patients responding with an anecdote involving their own furry friends. When I worked in the pediatrics area of the hospital, I discovered the best time to share pet adventures was during those frightening, sometimes painful procedures such as starting an IV or events calling for children to remain very still, such as a diagnostic scan. Especially during my rotation as a pediatric nurse, I would fantasize what it would be like to bring my pets in from home to really entertain the patients. At that time pet therapy had not made it to our rural hospital with 166 licensed beds. It was only a figment of my imagination.

In the spring of 2003, I received a call from Tammy, a lady in our community whom I had never met. I would soon discover that Tammy was successful as a Newfoundland breeder. She had also earned respect in the confirmation and obedience arenas in the dog show world. She started the conversation with, "Janet, are you the nurse who works at the hospital?" Before I could answer, she also asked, "And aren't you a huge dog lover?"

I hesitantly responded, "Yes," wondering where this conversation was leading. She then told me I would be the perfect candidate to start a pet therapy program at our hospital. Pet therapy? I immediately invited Tammy over to my place so I could hear more about this term, which was new to my vocabulary.

Tammy and I sat in my sunroom one gorgeous Saturday afternoon, and she began to explain why she and her 130-pound Newfoundland, Stowie, had begun to pursue pet therapy. She said she was fortunate to live next door to a wonderful retired couple with whom she and Stowie made frequent visits. She described her neighbors, the Barry's, as kind, honest people who appreciated the simple pleasures in life. On warm spring days after work, she and Stowie often found themselves sitting on their neighbors' front porch. Tammy chatted with them about everything imaginable. Stowie enjoyed their visits as much as Tammy, but eventually she would get restless and insist on heading home.

One particular day, the Barry's weren't the normal, cheerful couple with whom Tammy was accustomed to chatting. Mr. Barry appeared pale and tired after having gone through a battery of tests at the hospital due to a persistent cough and weight loss. He had a worried look and a solemn demeanor about him, and Tammy felt Stowie picked up on this change in behavior. Tammy thought to herself, why the hovering around Mr. Barry, and why is Stowie resistant to leave his side? On that day, Tammy had to literally drag Stowie home. She was a bit frustrated with her furry friend, who was typically much more willing and obedient to the requests of her owner.

The next day after work, Stowie was pacing at the door and abnormally anxious to return to the Barry's front porch. Tammy noticed that once they were on the Barry's porch, Stowie was extraordinarily tuned in to Mr. Barry, resting her head on the elderly gentleman's lap. Tammy commented, "Stowie, what's up with you lately?"

Mr. Barry spoke softly, as he and Stowie seemed to be in a trance. "Stowie, I see my soul in your eyes. You understood what was happening to me before I did." Mrs. Barry then shared their frightening news, that terminal lung cancer was Mr. Barry's final diagnosis with treatment starting next week. Mr. Barry then asked Tammy if Stowie could spend some extra time over at their place "just to be there for Kathryn (Mrs. Barry) and me" through the difficult times.

After this "ah-hah" moment with the Barry family, Tammy felt the need to share Stowie's ability to connect with people's emotional needs with the health care community. She planned to work with Stowie in preparation to "sit" for pet therapy certification, which is an extensive training program for pets and their owners. Pet therapy certification also requires a vigorous test for each pet therapy team as a culmination of much preparation and knowledge. "Certification helps to ensure that the animals will behave in a predictable manner."[1] This canine team assessment includes an intense focus on an array of human and environmental barriers that are typical in a health care setting. Without lots of training and exposure to the unique hospital environments, the average household pet would not thrive or even be comfortable around such distractions.

Over the next several days, my brain was racing with pet therapy ideas. Achieving certification for my dog and me as a pet therapy team would include a big commitment, but there was an overpowering thought that went along with this potential plan. This voluntary, free-of-charge canine service could be so beneficial for patients. There were multiple patients I interacted with every day at the hospital who could benefit from the simple yet impactful actions of a pet therapy team. Reflecting on even the patients I could recollect from that week, I could see some obvious opportunities to improve their hospital stay with pet therapy visits. My thoughts and imagination went a step further. What if Maggie, my Bernese Mountain Dog, were certified to see patients at the hospital? How would I go about selecting which patients would be appropriate for our visits?

The answers came so naturally they seemed to be a gift from God. The position I was functioning in at that time was as director of hospital supervision. The supervisors oversaw the flow of care on the inpatient areas. Each day I received a brief patient report and was made aware of those patients who had lengthy stays, limited family visits, or poor prognoses. Common sense told me that those types of patients could be the focus of a truly patient-centered pet therapy team. They were probably the patients who needed Maggie and me the most.

I started researching the unbelievable effects of pet therapy. Many true accounts supported the theory that often the sensitivity of animals to meet human needs goes against all reason. I also came to the realization that there might be animals out there that have a lot more skills to offer humans than we give them credit. It is the role of pet therapy advocates to create a medium in which those gifted creatures can function therapeutically.

As far as Tammy's initial proposition that I start up a pet therapy program in our hospital, I was truly inspired and totally focused on my new mission. Count me in, no question about it!

The Visit

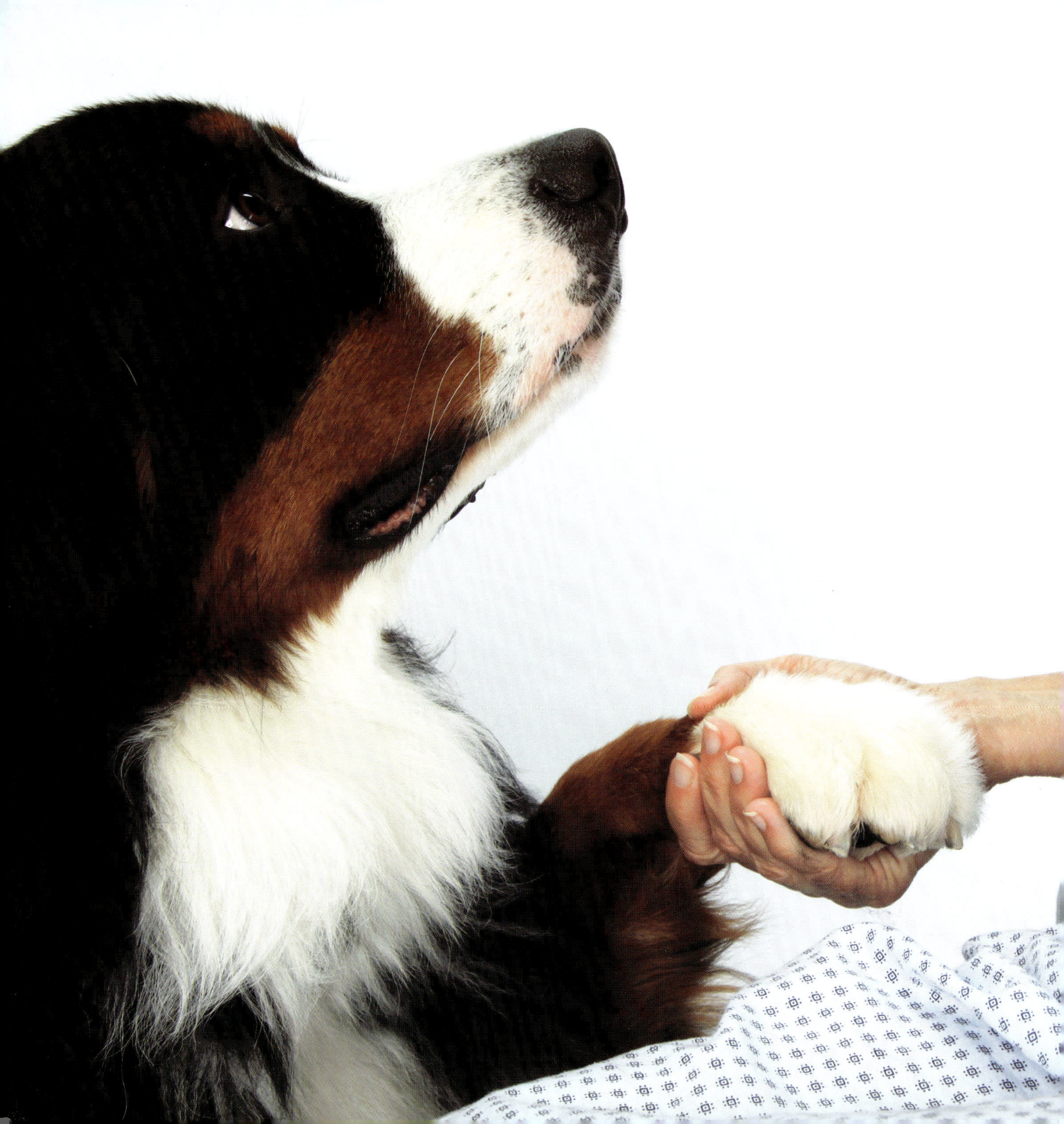

2
A BIT OF CONVINCING

It only took one conversation with a hospital administrator to realize that bringing pet therapy to our organization would require some convincing. I was told that the risk manager/safety officer would be the front line administrator to approach with my new-to-the-community concept. Being the detail-oriented person that I am, I prepared an organized proposal containing my pet therapy mission, objectives of the program, and an explanation of the logistics. I proudly handed it to the safety officer, who took one glance at it and said, "Janet, this sounds great." He paused before finishing his sentence. "For a nursing home, not a hospital." His quick response without even reading my proposal angered me. He had no clue how this program could positively affect the quality of the patients' stays. He must not have been aware that health care was experiencing a rising emphasis of including complimentary therapies into its culture.[1]

The therapeutic human-animal relationship has existed for thousands of years.[2] In 1859 even Florence Nightingale saw value in the healing powers of pets.[3] But I decided an adversarial approach wouldn't get pet therapy in the door. I began searching for some evidence that justified the value of this non-traditional care strategy for our traditional acute care facility. The research was extensive on the wonderful outcomes of programs in leading-edge hospitals such as Mayo Clinic, Northwestern University Hospital, and Children's Hospital in Michigan. When I resubmitted my proposal with this added research information, I made sure that each of the twelve articles I included had one word highlighted: HOSPITAL.

I wasn't aware at the time of the "incredible amount of work and collaboration" necessary to start up a pet therapy program—that "administration, risk management, legal, infection control and physicians must all be on the same page."[4] In my case, I would have to meet with representatives of several hospital entities to discuss my plan, answer their questions, and receive their approval. These interactions would take a considerable amount of time to accomplish.

After what seemed like eternity, the safety officer sent out on email to all of the administration that this new pet therapy program was approved but strictly as a trial. Any deviations from the newly created policy would lead to termination of the program. Since I was instrumental in building the policy and had a full understanding of the program, I was certain I wouldn't break any rules!

Reflecting on the safety officer's comments, I knew that my visits to patients with my dog Maggie would have to be huge customer satisfiers, win the physicians and staff over with this new concept, and never deviate from the guidelines. What I didn't realize at that time was that the safety officer did not share the same view as the hospital's open-minded leadership team. He found no personal value in pets and was allergic to animal dander. The last thing I would want was for anyone, patient or staff member, to have to go to the Emergency Department with an allergic reaction to Maggie's pet dander.

When drilling down to the specifics of the hospital's first involvement with pet therapy, I realized there are two avenues of healing that could be pursued. My intent was for the hospital startup program to consider both types of therapy and see what direction the needs of our patients would take us.

The first type of therapy, pet visitation, can be explained as short-term intervention in the form of social visits to patients.[5] The dog and handler spend time at the bedside communicating with the patient. Research has proven that these simple social visits have a lengthy list of therapeutic qualities. They can satisfy patients' need to nurture, be accepted by another living being, direct thoughts outside of their illness concerns, exercise their socialization skills, and nourish their need for physical contact and support relaxation.[6]

The second type of pet therapy is animal-assisted work in which animals are used to facilitate a specific cognitive or physical function.[7] This type of intervention often involves measurable results. Some goal-oriented activities include speech and physical therapy, ventilator weaning, self-esteem improvement, post trauma support, and bedside motivation. Assistance the dog and handler team might offer in animal-assisted work would include comfort, emotional reassurance, and motivation to the patient.

At the same time I was involved in arranging the hospital program, my 12-month-old Bernese Mountain Dog Maggie's education moved into the fast lane. Maggie loved any kind of attention. No matter if it was attending dog obedience school, a.k.a. doggie school, working to improve her obedience skills on the driveway, or practicing greeting people at the local Walmart or Cracker Barrel, it was all about Maggie. Through training, my eighty-five pound puppy that was full of energy and loved the entire human race was turning into a consistently calm, focused, and compassionate canine.

Obedience school came easy for both of us. Maggie was my fifth dog to take through the local program, she picked up the information quickly, and we were diligent about our homework. Maggie ended up being the valedictorian of her class. It didn't hurt that the rewards for good behavior were treats. Maggie, like most of us women, was food driven.

A Bit Of Convincing

After passing obedience school, Maggie's second test was to become certified as a Canine Good Citizen. The American Kennel Club sponsors this title to encourage dogs to act like well-mannered citizens out in public. Maggie sailed through that course and graduation exercise.

The biggest validation of pet therapy readiness was the actual therapy dog certification, which I chose to do through a nationally recognized organization. Of the list of approximately fifteen testing items, our challenges fell in two categories. First, therapy dogs were to ignore any food patients may have in front of them when making their visits. To test for this ability, a plate of food was placed in front of the dog applicant, and the expectation was for the dog to leave it alone. As I mentioned earlier, eating was one of Maggie's favorite activities. Keep in mind that at her height, a patient's bedside tray and food was at her eye level. So I started her training by leaving food about five feet from her, and I gradually worked my way to positioning it right under her nose. Maggie learned to leave it until I told her, "Okay."

Our other challenge came with the requirement for her to remain calm and in a down position for several minutes with me, her handler, out of site. She and I had grown very close through all of her training and pampering; therefore, she was a little uneasy at first to see me disappear from her view, especially in an unfamiliar setting. We practiced this skill in

Maggie and I preparing for certification

10

different locations other than home, and in each exercise I included a longer timeframe of me, the handler, being out of sight.

Fortunately Maggie passed her therapy dog certification, and I was one proud handler. Our next task was to begin preparation for our very first patient visit as a pet therapy team!

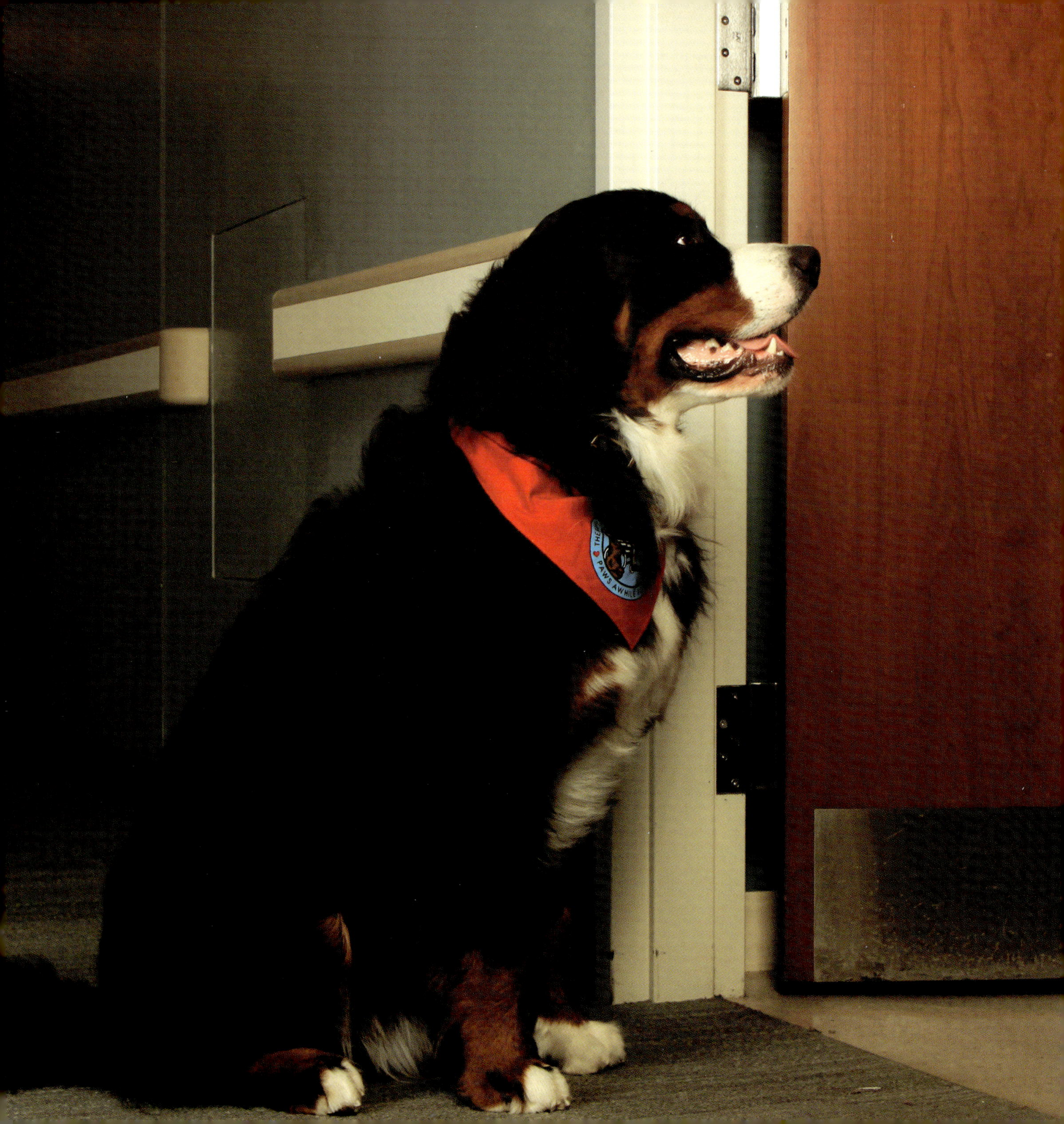
PAWS AWHILE

3
ONE PAW IN THE DOOR

The time had finally arrived for our first visit. Our completed "to do" list included leadership approval, therapy dog certification, therapy dog health records turned into Human Resources, and one very large and fluffy, freshly bathed therapy dog. Oh yes, there was one more item on that list: an anxious therapy dog handler. I had been copied on the e-mail that had been composed by the safety officer and sent to hospital leaders urging them to be watchful and to report any mishaps.

For the "maiden voyage" of pet visitation, I had carefully selected a list of patients who I thought would benefit from the experience. With the list folded neatly in my pocket, I entered the hospital and followed the hallway path that the safety officer had designated. Even before Maggie and I arrived upstairs where the inpatients stay, we had numerous employees stop us. One physician in particular got down on one knee, gave Maggie a vigorous pat, and expressed his appreciation

A welcoming pat from a physician

that we would be visiting his patients. Concerned that Maggie's demeanor would be monitored, I was hopeful the physician didn't evoke too much enthusiasm from my calm natured, but rookie, therapy dog.

A couple of nurses also drew near with smiling faces and said, "Your dog is too cool. Are the nurses allowed to get a little lovin' too?" Maggie, who thrived on attention, offered them her paw per my command. Their response and the resulting commotion over the hospital's new concept of allowing a real, live dog into the building began to attract the attention of visitors and patients walking in the halls. Though Maggie and I showed our appreciation, I certainly didn't want to create a loud, disturbing scenario for patients who were trying to rest, so we moved on quickly.

As we approached our destination, I heard a patient in a room say, "I could have sworn I just saw a dog walk by." I was amused by that comment that I soon learned would echo often from patient rooms.

I'd selected Mrs. Ray for our first visit because she had appeared really down when I was at her bedside earlier that day. She'd made very little eye contact and spoke in a monotone voice. I tried to kid around with her and at least stimulate a smile but was unsuccessful. When I thanked her for allowing me to start her difficult IV, I asked her if she was a dog lover. Her response was, "Well, sure I am. I've always had a dog." She then gave me permission to bring Maggie in, but I gathered no sense of pleasure in her response or observed any change in her expression. To prepare for the visit, I confirmed that Mrs. Ray was clear of any infectious illness, immunosuppression, and pet allergies. I also obtained the permission of her covering physician to receive a therapy dog visit.

I was glad to see some family members at her side when I knocked on the door. Maybe they would become engaged in our visit, which might stimulate Mrs. Ray. To my surprise, when the patient laid eyes on us, she raised the head of her bed and told her family that she and I had made plans for a visit earlier in the day. It tickled me that for the first time her voice had some inflection and a hint of a positive demeanor.

All present marveled at Maggie's beauty and behavior. I proceeded to explain her breed, our preparation, and our mission. The conversation became very interactive as Mrs. Ray and her family reminisced about all the animals they remembered as they were growing up. By the time we left, she had told me about her pets, asked us to repeat some of our silly pet tricks, and thanked us several times for coming. The very best news of all, from a professional point of view, was that Mrs. Ray was quite engaged in our visit. The change in her demeanor was visible to all. At the end of our visit, one of her sons walked us to the door and expressed his appreciation for our time.

Maggie and I were warmly welcomed by the three other patients on my list. With our visit so well received by Mrs. Ray, we entered the next rooms in a more confident fashion. During our dialogues with patients, I noticed some of the staff members peeking their heads in the patient rooms as to assess the patients' reaction to this new type of bedside offering. It seemed the nurses personally enjoyed our visits and were excited to discover a new adjunct care for their patients. As we spent time in those other three rooms, Maggie and I experienced a variety of positive patient responses ranging from soft-spoken gestures of appreciation to boisterous laughter and heart-warming conversations about the patients' own pets. One other optimistic thought summarized our evening: in the words of the safety officer, we'd had "no mishaps."

As the elevator door closed to take us back downstairs, Maggie and I had the first of many elevator "conversations." I kneeled down and gave my fuzzy partner a hug. "Wow, we did it! Actually, Maggie, YOU did it. I'm so proud of you." Maggie, not I, had ever so briefly stepped into the world of these patients. I was acting only as Maggie's assistant, a backdrop for her healing work. Maggie had displayed her simple and entertaining gestures, and they had facilitated an about-face in Mrs. Ray's mood. My furry friend had created a healthy diversion from Mrs. Ray's worrisome medical concerns. How could I describe to others how I had observed Maggie succeeding where I had failed earlier in the day? Together we'd completed our first healing moments.

I thought about our first experience while driving home. There were so many lessons learned. The four patients we saw were of various ages with differing personalities and a variety of diagnoses. Some had visitors in the room while we were there and others were alone with us. The common factor was that they all seemed to embrace our visit. Another observation: I was pleasantly surprised at the interest shown by our physicians and employees. Although our interactions with staff were time intensive, they were value added.

As a health care provider myself, I realized that these care givers function in a very stressful environment. Research has proven that pet therapy can impact the attitudes of staff and lead to improved interaction with patients. Canine interaction with both the patients and the staff can "enable the staff to maximize their time with a patient via a shared experience and decreases staff stress levels."[1] So if Maggie and I could assist in making staff members' days more pleasant through pet visitation, there would be an added bonus to our work.

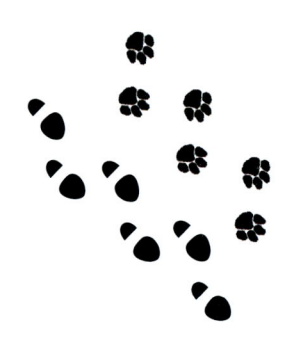

The Visit

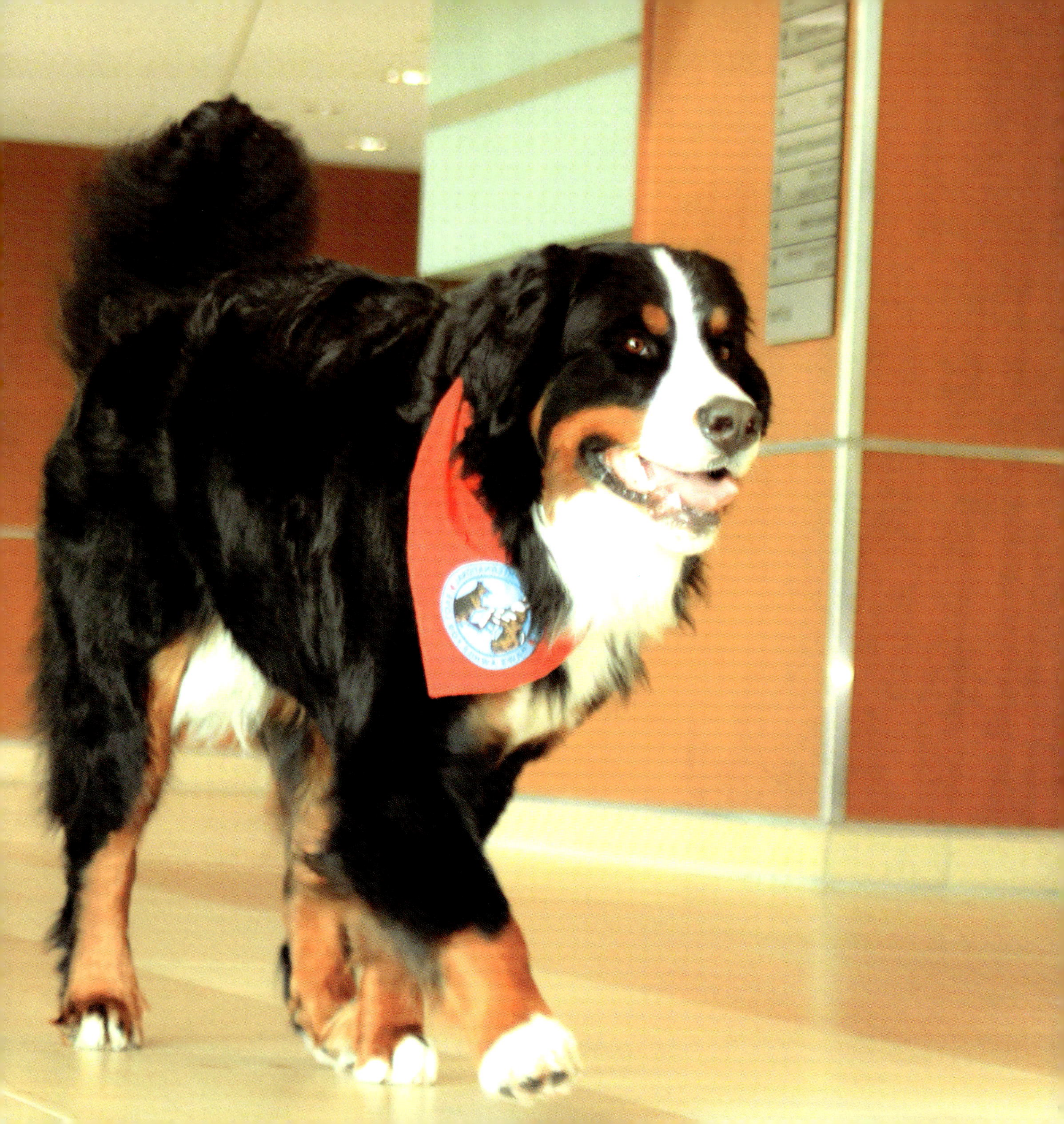

4
GETTING RIGHT TO WORK

Working three 12-hour shifts a week, I had the time I needed to make lots of therapy visits on my days off. Maggie became a pro, and she truly enjoyed coming to "work" with me. She was not a natural barker, but she expressed her excitement every time we loaded up my car with her bag containing her pet trick props. I kidded the patients receiving our service that Maggie's job status was part-time—little work, no benefits— and occasionally she was caught sleeping on the job.

Over time Maggie realized exactly why she was entering a patient room, and my main responsibility was simply to take her there. She became an expert at understanding what each patient needed. She knew when to be serious, entertaining, or empathetic. Patient after patient, trip after trip, she helped patients relax and lower their anxiety, distracted them from their worries, and boosted their morale. She was demonstrating what one author explained, that the dogs arrive in the location where they are to administer pet therapy, they understand their job, and their whole demeanor adapts to their therapy dog role.[1]

I learned to listen carefully to the verbal cues and pay attention to the facial expressions in our patients in order to understand exactly how we could serve them best. Some patients were interested in hearing all about pet therapy and my dog. Others wanted to be entertained with our comical pet tricks. And there were more reserved patients who simply wanted to pet Maggie or share a hug. One gentleman requested that Maggie get on his bed. When I told him that this practice wasn't allowed at the hospital, he suggested that I shut his door.

I tried to learn from our experiences and make our visits more effective. For instance, I noticed that many of our larger, bedfast patients couldn't really get positioned in bed so that they had eye contact with Maggie and could pet her. So I purchased a little red stool that I often carried with me. I also taught Maggie to put her front paws on the side rails of a wheelchair, again, so that patients could interact more closely with her. She learned to rest her head wherever I placed my open hand. This action seemed to eliminate any initial intimidating notions on the part of the patient she was visiting, and gave her a submissive appearance.

Patients seemed to love watching Maggie perform tricks. As a result, our selection of entertaining bedside antics grew over time. We tried anything that might elicit a giggle. For example, I ran across a stuffed children's toy that was a telephone. I would tell patients that every working woman like Maggie kept connected with a phone, and then I would make the phone ring. Maggie would pick it up and toss it to me. I also would tell patients that Maggie and I jogged together and both warmed up before we ran. We would then stretch our legs out in unison. I taught her to respond to my fake sneeze by pulling a handkerchief

Maggie retrieved this message from her bag

out of a tissue box. And we added a "say your prayers" action to our repertoire in which Maggie would lay across the little red stool and bow her head.

Patients often commented that they wished their loved ones were present when we visited. So we created a token of our visit that would stimulate conversation when their family members arrived. I taught Maggie to end our visits by pulling a hollow tube out of her bag and offering a scrolled "get well" greeting I'd prepared in advance to give to the patients. I would see these greetings on bedside tables and taped to IV poles later when I'd make rounds as a supervisor.

Another lesson learned in our early days of patient visitation was how fatiguing pet visitation is on a therapy dog. After a couple hours of interacting with patients exhibiting a variety of personalities and in settings with multiple stimuli such as IV pump alarms and cardiac monitor noises, Maggie would become exhausted. It was my role to keep her from reaching that point, which would result in her no longer being able to interact effectively with patients. When my husband would arrive home after work to find Maggie in a deep sleep, he would make kidding comments such as, "Let me guess. Maggie had a hard day at the hospital."

One tired therapy dog

Maggie and I visited with many hospice patients after I found research documenting that canine visits are quite therapeutic for these terminally ill patients and their families. Research indicates that these visits provide an outlet for the patients' intense stress.[2] We called on one lovely, elderly patient named Mary several times due to the positive feedback we received from her family. She had beautiful grey hair, and her daughters were frequently arranging it for her. Mary's inpatient stay occurred at the same time Maggie and I were approached for a local newspaper interview on pet therapy, so I asked Mary if she would be a part of our photo shoot. She so looked forward to the photographer coming to her bedside that she had her daughters come in and make sure her hair was just right for the occasion.

We began to see a pattern to our visits. Family members would approach us in the halls even before we entered the rooms and often tell me their loved ones could really use some cheering up that day. Patients we'd visited on earlier occasions welcomed us enthusiastically to come again to their bedside. They embraced our conversations and graciously allowed Maggie's charismatic presence to brighten their day. We were humbled to provide a medium for a cheerful moment.

Requests for visits grew, and customer service surveys reflected patient support of this non-traditional addition to patient care. The feedback we received mirrored the conclusion of one researcher who stated, "The importance of animals in people's lives has been recognized. As a work assistant or special companion, the contribution of animals to enhance the quality of human life has been occurring for thousands of years."[3] These informal and unstructured visits can impact children, adults, mental health patients, and those with

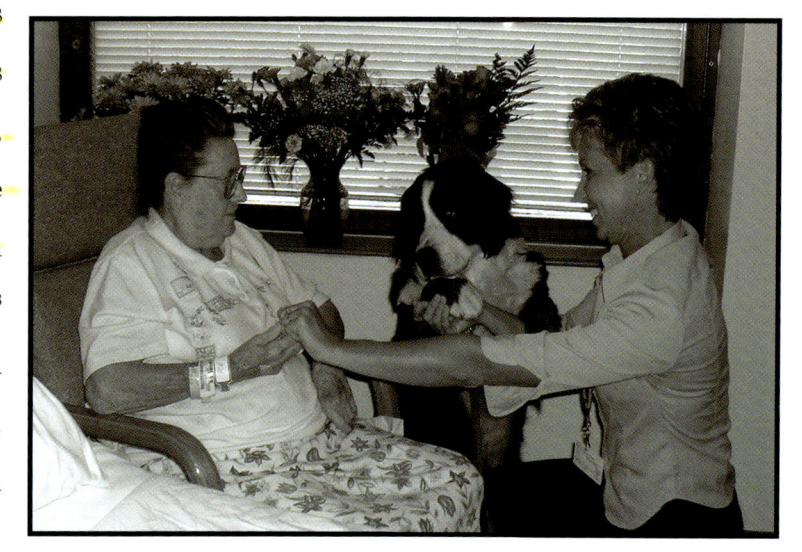

Mary and Maggie

disabilities. That same researcher described pet visitation as a "holistic approach for individual and family rehabilitation."[4]

Maggie and I had only one experience of rejection. I recall a family member recruiting us in the hall to visit her mother. Maggie walked in the room, stared at the patient, and turned so her back was to the patient. I was initially embarrassed and quite shocked. She'd never acted in such a way. Then I heard the patient say to her daughter, "You know I don't like dogs. What is this about?" Apparently not only can "canine therapists" figure out what patients need, but also what they don't need. As one researcher stated, pets are not for everyone, and in fact some patients may become quite uncomfortable in their presence; therefore, visiting these individuals can even increase their stress level.[5]

Many pet therapy organizations insure all visits and events that occur in relation to the therapy work. The sole visit-related injury the occurred to Maggie and me happened while visiting with a petite and frail ninety-year-old resident of one of the nursing homes. She asked Maggie to shake, so Maggie simply plopped her big paw across the lady's lap. In that innocent response, her paw accidentally scraped the top of the woman's very thin-skinned hand, which led to a small abrasion. I felt terrible and apologized profusely. The patient's daughter wasn't upset, and she said the benefit of our visit far outweighed the minor injury. It came in handy to be a nurse, as I assisted the staff in dressing the woman's wound.

One other memorable event happened in those early days of pet visitation. As we were walking down the hall at the hospital, we met up with the security guard in passing. Maggie stared closely at him and let out a huge bark, which is prohibited. I started to scold her, but then I realized why she had responded as she did. Just days before, as I was standing in my front yard with Maggie, a UPS truck pulled up. The delivery man approached me. Maggie didn't bark or show any aggressive moves, but the delivery man was obviously uncomfortable with her presence. He pitched the small package into my chest, turned quickly, and jumped back into his truck. All of the sudden, Maggie cried and started wiping her nose on the ground. When she looked up at me, I realized that he had pepper sprayed her. Never was I more angry. That UPS man had been wearing a brown uniform very similar to the one the security guard in the hall was wearing. Not just humans learn from past experiences.

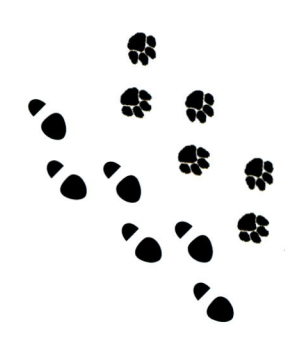

THE VISIT

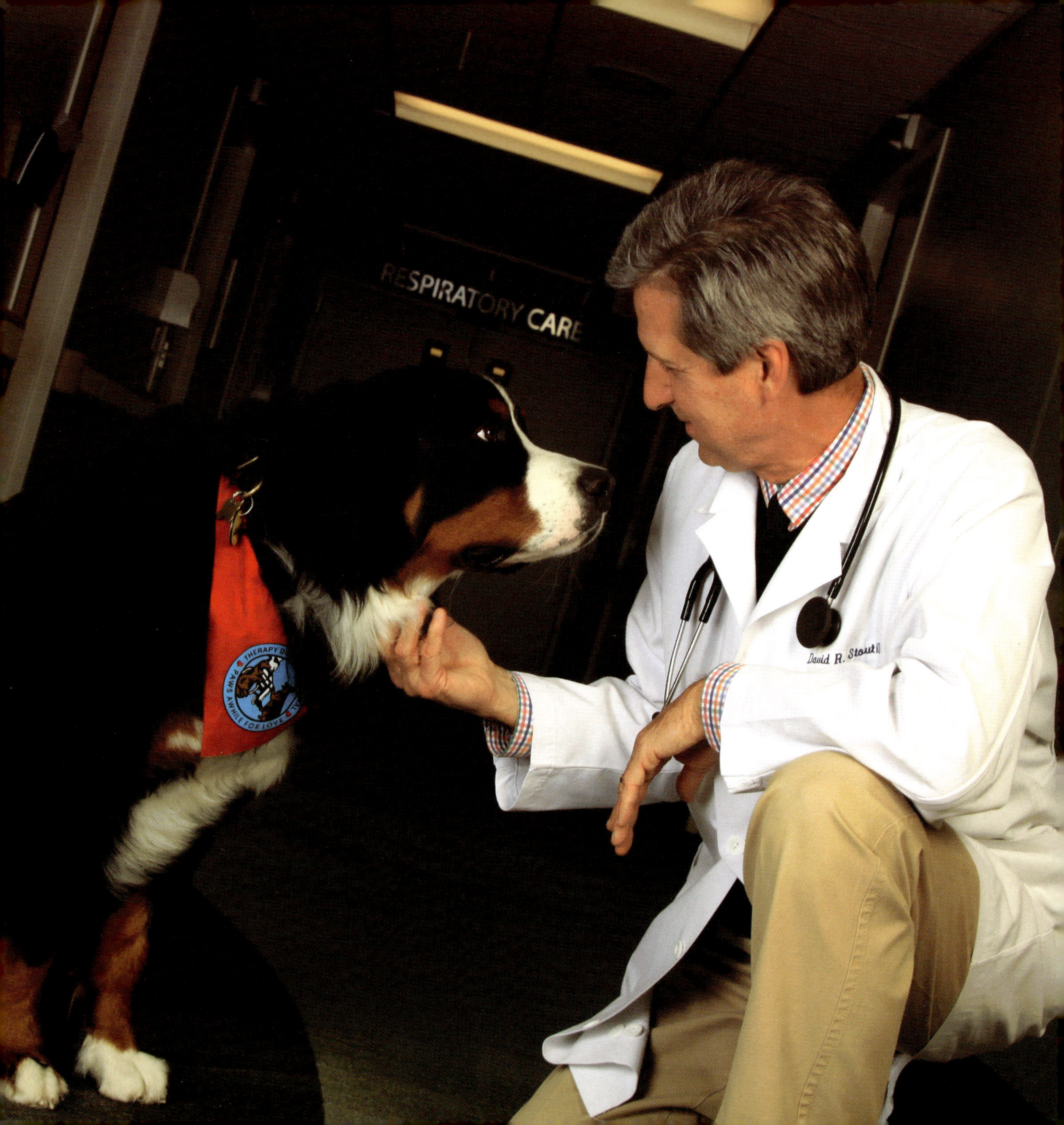
RESPIRATORY CARE
David R. Stout
PAWS AWHILE FOR LOVE

5
SPREADING THE WORD

The hospital's pet therapy program had been up and running for several months. This new patient offering was receiving some great feedback from patients and their families. The word was spreading. One day as Maggie and I were just about to head upstairs, I heard an overhead page to call the operator. A reporter from the local newspaper was on the phone. The hospital had contacted the newspaper and requested press coverage on our new program. After accepting the request for an interview and photo shoot, I shared my excitement over the big news with Maggie as the elevator door closed. "Wow, Mag, maybe we are making a difference. I guess pet therapy is officially accepted."

The resulting front-page newspaper article was titled, "Hospital Patients PAWS for a Visit." The hospital staff and I were most appreciative of the coverage. It gave our community awareness of the program's existence and how to request visitations if the need arose. The article also spurred community groups to learn more about pet therapy. Within a few weeks, I had a couple of speaking engagement requests on the calendar, and I started preparing a PowerPoint presentation. It would reveal the explosion of new evidence that supported our work and share some heartfelt encounters of patients receiving these first visits. Pet therapy, as one researcher put it, "has grown from home experimentation to research-supported utilization in health care settings."[1] My message in that first newspaper article and eventually in my presentations included evidence of the physical, psychological, and social impact these "canine interventionists" contribute to human health.

The Bernese Mountain Dog Club of America extended an invitation for me to speak at its National Specialty in Frankenmuth, Michigan. It would be fun, I thought, to present to peers that share the same passion about this breed and to educate them on how terrific this breed is in filling the role of pet therapy dog. At the event, which was attended by both dog owners and their dogs, the breed's mild-tempered, calm, people-loving spirit provided the perfect backdrop for my talk. Their spectacular markings and warm, fuzzy appearance attracted even those who weren't huge dog lovers.

The state nurses association invited me to present at its Southern Indiana meeting—with Maggie, or course. It was a privilege to share this alternative, supplemental approach to managing pain, anxiety, and stress with a room full of patient advocates. I included supporting evidence described by a team of advanced practice nurses. Their research explained the value of animal-assisted therapy in promoting quality of life and positive health benefits.[2]

On the evening of the presentation, Maggie and I were asked to wait in a nearby room used for nursing education. We walked into this holding area, and my eyes scanned to see the perfect place for us to wait. But Maggie's attention was drawn to the mannequin in the bed. She looked at it, back at me, perked up, and wagged her tail. She was unleashed, so she walked briskly on her own up to the bedside. The "patient" did not respond to her presence. She looked back at me in disbelief and then nudged the mannequin's hand with her nose. Still no

Second grade students meet Maggie

response, so she walked around to the other side of the bed, all the time staring at the mannequin. I couldn't help but chuckle at her persistent attempt to interact with this most unfriendly resemblance of a patient that had captured her attention. Finally I just had to say, "Maggie, I don't think this guy appreciates your friendly gestures. It's okay, girl."

I have spoken to several youth organizations including 4-H, Brownie troops, and Junior Leaders as well. Knowing that relationships with animals often lead to healthier human-to-human interactions, I have tried to instill this message in young people of all ages. Animals in their homes have lots to offer their families and perhaps others, if given the opportunity.

Maggie and I also have given presentations at many schools and explained the benefits of our mission in health care. We often demonstrate a "mock" bedside visit by pretending that one of the students is our patient. Our school talks typically end with each child meeting Maggie.

I've always thought a health care background was helpful for individuals desiring to visit patients with a dog, regardless of the settings for the visits. As a nurse, I was already aware of the patient health factors that precluded a dog's presence such as pet hair allergies, immunosuppression (which lowers a person's ability to fight off infection), isolation cases, open or uncovered wounds, and open tracheostomies. My nursing experience also gave me a huge awareness of the absolute necessity of respecting patient confidentiality. The therapy dog organizations that certify therapy dog teams have done a great job of providing education on topics related to visit safety and risk.

A big squeeze for the camera

SPREADING THE WORD

I decided not to do any visits when the Joint Commission, the hospital's regulatory agency that allows it to keep its doors open, came for an inspection and evaluation of compliance with health care guidelines. After the exit interview was over, one of the hospital's pathologists relayed this story to me. The inspector was complimentary of the cleanliness of our facility and the forward thinking leadership team. He also said, "I'm surprised I haven't seen any pet therapy taking place around here."

The physicians at the hospital grew to be very supportive of the pet therapy program, proving what one author has stated. "Once physicians see the interactions, they will be persuaded to try the program."[3] One of the physicians gave us permission to see all of his patients. When I questioned him about those with allergies, he kiddingly said, "They can all have Benadryl." The personnel working in Intensive Care welcomed Maggie and me for visits in their unit. A few members of this respected team even had their photo taken with her. They were surprised that she cooperated with this wheelchair pose and chuckled when she didn't want to jump out after the photo was taken.

One of the younger surgeons always met Maggie and me with a smile and would ask if we were seeing any of his patients. As I would watch him "rough her up" and "let his hair down" with her, I wondered if Maggie was providing him with a needed, stress-free moment after finishing a mentally taxing surgical procedure. A more senior physician thanked us for

Hangin' out in Intensive Care

seeing his patients. He had read of the positive attributes of pet therapy. Because of the information he had acquired, he felt our pet visits offered a valuable service.

The local nursing staff also appreciated and supported Maggie and me tremendously. The nurses began assessing their patients for visit appropriateness. Maggie's happy demeanor seemed to be contagious as she brought many smiles to hard-working staff members. The nurses would often make a brief appearance in their patients' rooms during Maggie's visit, perhaps taking in a bit of therapy themselves. In return for her hard work, Maggie received many gestures of appreciation from the staff in the form of dog treats of all kinds. During our visits, it was not uncommon for staff members and visitors to ask for a cell phone photo shot of them with Maggie.

Over and over again, Maggie and I were blessed with pet therapy opportunities. Numerous physicians and staff were responding positively to our mission, patients and families were requesting our visits, and the community was spreading the word.

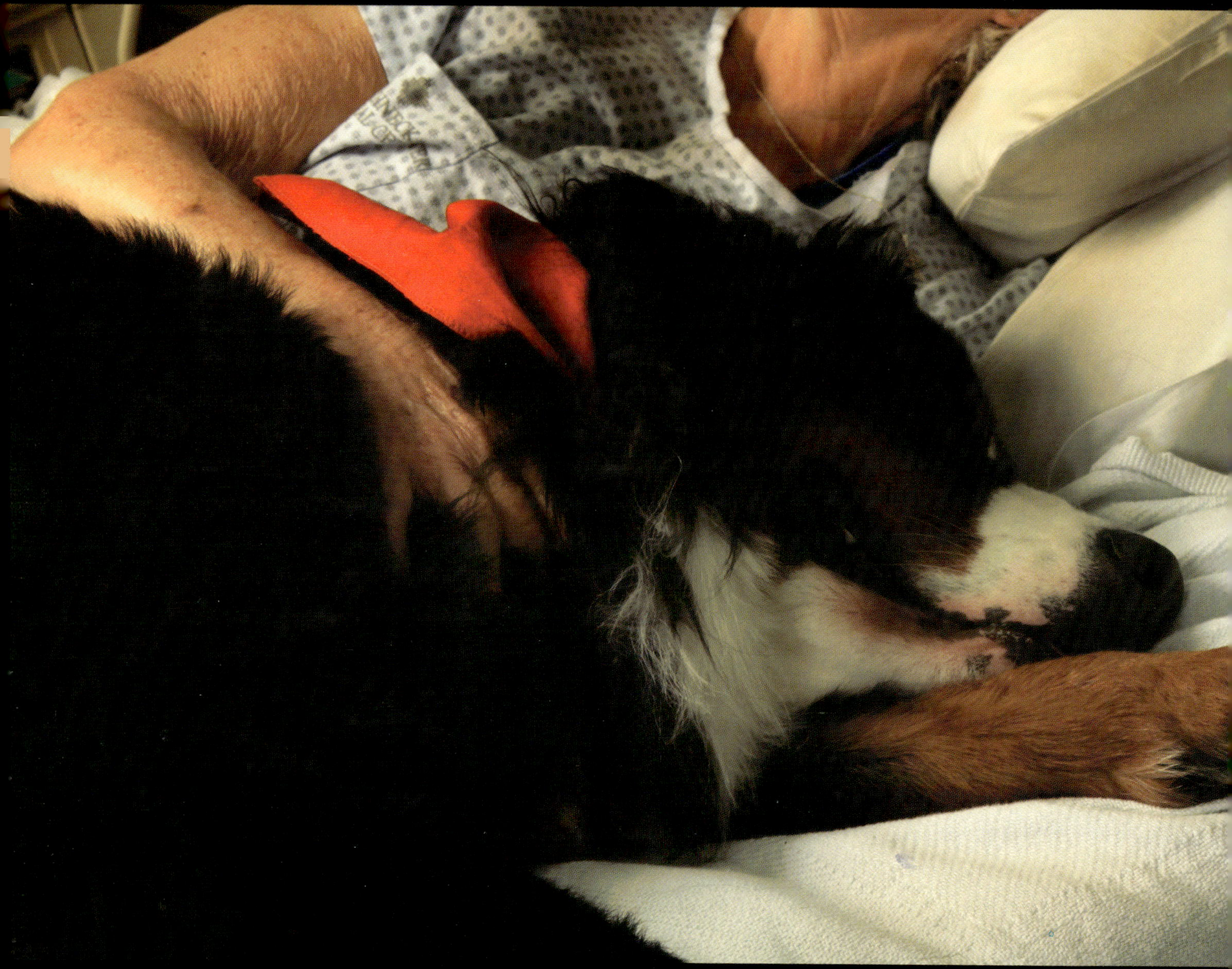

6
WHEN YOU'RE WITH ME

Since I had received the patient report at shift change from the night shift supervisor that morning, I couldn't stop thinking about one patient in particular whose cancer had spread to her bones. The progression of her disease had greatly increased her level of pain, and she had very little family to support and comfort her through this devastating illness. Norma sounded like a perfect candidate for pet therapy.

Prior to Maggie visiting Norma, we checked in at the nurses' station, as the hospital had specified in its pet therapy policy. Norma's physician had given approval for a pet therapy visit. Norma had no health related concerns in her medical history or admitting diagnosis that would preclude her from a visit. I had also verified with her nurses that Norma would be interested in seeing us.

When Maggie and I entered Norma's room, we found a very pale, frail, weak, 90-pound lady in her sixties. Her face lit up when we walked in the room. As Norma stared at Maggie, she told her she was the most beautiful dog she had ever seen. She wanted to know all about Maggie and what pet therapy had to offer. She didn't want to talk about her own issues; she was simply infatuated with my dog.

I explained what breed Maggie was, the history behind the breed, and about Maggie's role at the hospital. The whole time I talked, Norma stroked Maggie's silky hair. She expressed a desire for her niece to meet Maggie, but the niece wasn't coming until tomorrow. Recalling that the nurses had said this lady had very little family or other visitors, I offered to return the next day with Maggie and meet her niece.

I didn't usually visit the same patient two consecutive days, but I had a feeling that Norma really needed a positive focus in her life. So the next day, as we stepped off the elevator, a pleasant lady was standing outside Norma's room. She noticed Maggie. "You've got to be Maggie," she said and then turned her eyes to me. "My Aunt Norma called last night, and this dog is all she talked about."

I humbly accepted her kind words and said we were looking forward to visiting her aunt again. Norma's niece had come to finalize plans to transfer her aunt to a nursing home the next day. Due to Norma's terminal state, the niece said she would be introducing her aunt to the hospice program. How sad, I thought. We have to brighten this lady's day!

Maggie and I certainly tried. She performed all of her pet tricks and had Norma and her niece chuckling away. It was a rewarding visit for Maggie and me as well. As we said our good-byes, I asked Norma if she would enjoy a visit from us in the nursing home. She seemed very interested, so I told her to expect us. Maggie looked at me as we walked into the elevator as if to say, "I didn't know we had privileges for pet therapy there." I thought, *We don't, but we will soon.*

I gave Norma a few days to get settled in her new environment, which was an extended care facility located in a town about twenty minutes from the hospital. I then called that nursing home's director of nursing to explain my mission, our credentials as a pet therapy team, and my intent. I explained how Norma seemed to benefit emotionally from our hospital visits, and so Maggie and I hoped to provide further therapy for her. The director, in turn, explained the facility's policy on pet visitation. It was much more relaxed than the hospital's policy, and I was confident that Maggie would interact well with Norma in this environment.

THE VISIT

Five days after our last visit with Norma in the hospital, Maggie and I made our way to the nursing home. The nurses at the facility welcomed us, and they voiced their concern over the fact that they were challenged to keep Norma's pain under control. "She's had a rough day today," Norma's nurse elaborated, "so I'm sure she'll be glad to see you."

I let Maggie enter the room in front of me to surprise Norma. She was lying flat in bed but rolled over with outstretched arms when she saw us enter her room. "There you are, you big, pretty thing," she said softly. Maggie's tail was wagging as if she'd just met up with an old friend. While the two of them reunited, my eyes scanned Norma's modest surroundings. On her dresser was the picture that I had given her of Maggie on our first visit.

The three of us visited awhile. Then Maggie began staring at Norma as if she was planning how she could best care for her. Was she sensing Norma's level of discomfort? Maggie proceeded to do something I'd never encouraged or allowed during a therapy session. She carefully placed her huge front paws on Norma's bed. I was just about to discipline her when Norma said, "Maggie, I think you want to come up here and cuddle with me. I would like that." Norma scooted over to make room.

I immediately questioned that idea, since Maggie weighed more than this fragile, petite lady. This activity was not allowed in the hospital. On the other hand, the nursing home's policy did not forbid it. I had learned earlier in my conversation with the director that nursing homes were often more lenient about pet visits.

Norma was quite persistent with her idea, so I put a bath towel down on the bed and motioned to Maggie. She carefully maneuvered herself onto the bed. My furry, gentle giant then lowered herself in slow motion, as if she understood the need not to harm her new friend. Norma started stroking Maggie's fur just as she had done in the hospital. But this time Norma's eyes were closed. She then made a remark I'll never forget. "Maggie, when you're with me, my bones don't hurt." The

35

next several minutes in Norma's room were ones of poignant silence. The only movement was Norma petting Maggie's back.

On three more occasions, Maggie and I visited Norma and made the most of our time to "cuddle" (as Norma put it) before she passed on. Norma's comment that Maggie lessened her pain validated some research that pet therapy can assist in pain relief. It offers a complimentary therapy with less bothersome and dangerous adverse effects than many pain medications. Petting animals releases endomorphine, the body's natural pain suppressor.[1]

Without question, I had been blessed once again to observe some powerful yet very simple moments of healing. The interaction I witnessed between Norma and Maggie was the catalyst that would lead us to surge forward confidently with our mission. There were numerous patients yet to visit who would benefit from the compassionate actions of my four-legged therapist.

THE VISIT

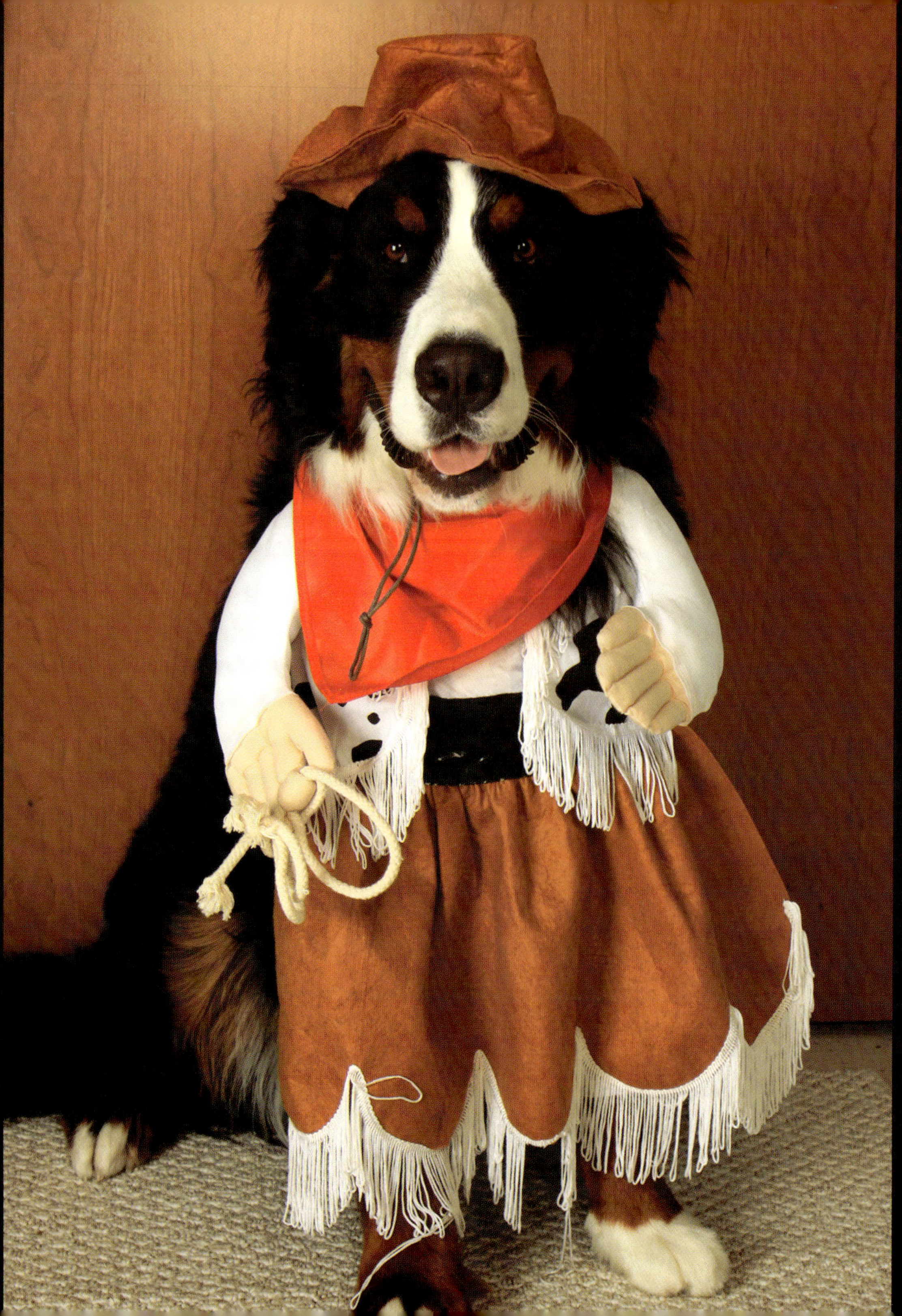

7
PLAYTIME IN PEDIATRICS

It never seemed right that children had to be sick enough to be in the hospital. So in my former pediatric nursing days, I did my best to make their stay a pleasant experience. Fun-loving, gamelike approaches to necessary nursing interventions helped lower the anxiety of these young patients, but my best solution for improving the hospital experience for these children was against hospital policy. No dogs were allowed in the hospital at that time. I admit I was one of those nurses who envisioned smuggling in a pet to cheer the children up during their stay. That was long before I knew about pet therapy.

Although I didn't realize it at the time, my family pet while growing up provided me with frequent emotional support. While my parents were at work, my grandmother cared for my brother and me. I was quite intimidated by her gruff, assertive voice. I would find myself retreating to the comfort of my empathetic and consoling Shetland sheep dog named Tammy. She seemed to understand me and would snuggle up with me and make me feel better. I also found support and daytime

My personal childhood experience with pet therapy

companionship with my neighbor's collie, Buster, so I would bring him in our house while everyone was at work. Tammy and Buster appeared sensitive to my feelings, probably decreased my anxiety, and were a constant source of security.

As I became involved in pediatric health care, I thought back on those days and wondered if the same benefits I received from pets could be offered to our pediatric patients who were feeling insecure while out of their comfort zone. One author of a nursing publication article summarized what many pediatric nurses and I now know from firsthand experience. "I don't think any nurse needs to be told how good it (pet therapy) is for their (pediatric) patients. It just makes their day. It changes everything. For those few minutes, it takes their minds off the procedure or their pain or the fact that they're not home … I can't say enough about it."[1] Pet therapy assists these patients through a difficult time in some of the same ways it did for me as a child.

Maggie and I began visiting patients in the pediatric unit soon after our first adult patient pet therapy visit. Maggie loved being in pediatrics as much as the children loved her. She probably exerted more physical energy and worked harder with the children than with the other patients, but she loved every second of it. She exhibited a fun disposition and performed her tricks well. One could almost detect a smile on her face when she was on the pediatric unit. Her enviable bedside manners, teddy bear appearance, and silly pet tricks brought excitement and

Mikayla and Maggie—all smiles

smiles to children of all ages. Research has proven that pet therapy creates significant improvements in the mood and happiness in the pediatric patient.[2]

One day we went to the pediatric unit to visit a ten-year-old girl named Kiley who had been hospitalized for several days. When we knocked on Kiley's door to greet her, I could see that she had been sitting and watching for us from her bedside chair. She was a pitiful site as she was hooked up to an IV in her arm, oxygen through her nose, and electrodes on her chest for a respiratory monitor. Despite being very ill with pneumonia, Kiley became so excited when she saw us that she leaped across her bed and gave Mag a hug. Fortunately Kiley's IV tubing, oxygen tubing, and monitor apparatus came with her, and no harm was done. The visit went very well, even better than I'd imagined. Kiley's mother and her nurses too commented that Maggie's visit had encouraged a more playful, happy mood in Kiley.

Maggie and I made several visits to tonsillectomy patients, which proved to be helpful in their post-operative recovery. I recall a three-year-old youngster fresh from surgery who refused to cooperate. He would not let the nurses see in his mouth to check for bleeding or monitor his vital signs. Nor would he accept sips of liquids. When the nurses saw us coming, they told this little guy, "There's a big, fluffy dog that's come to play with you if you open your mouth for us and take some sips." Mesmerized by Maggie, he failed to realize that his vital signs were being taken or that he was sipping from his

Emma and Maggie share hugs

cup. This little fellow was a perfect example of how therapy dogs can create a therapeutic conduit to assist in patient care.[3]

At first I was hesitant to have Maggie around toddlers just learning to walk. Her wagging tail could knock them off balance. One toddler's mother invited us into her room. Maggie and I stood at her door as I expressed my concern. "Are you sure you want us to come in?" I asked. Maggie had received no direction from me as to how to approach the toddler, but she proceeded to lie down on the floor and crawl into the room. Some dogs have great intuitive skills. I was blessed to own one.

Visits to pediatrics were not without challenges. As one journalist explains, "It's imperative to be watchful of allergies, those who have seizures due to high levels of excitement and those with aggressive tendencies."[4] Also, researchers warn that "just as not every animal is a suitable partner for an animal assisted program, so too, not every child is an appropriate candidate for this type of intervention."[5] I had spent a tremendous amount of time building trust with my dog. I wanted her to know that no matter what I asked of her, she was not going to be harmed. If we were in the presence of an aggressive patient, we would maintain our distance. There were a couple of occasions where children reacted quickly in striking at Maggie or grabbing her, and I felt bad that I didn't anticipate those moves coming.

In pediatrics there are many psychological applications for pet therapy dogs. As a former pediatric nurse, I remember some of the family dynamics that could occur. There might be a mother, stepfather, stepmother, and father in the room with the patient during pet visitation. Pet therapy creates a socially accepted conversation piece that can build bridges in troubled relationships. One author believes animals lessen family pressures, act as a buffer during conflict, and improve family dynamics.[6] Pets also display compassion, which can be later used in human-to-human relationships. Additionally, animals offer unconditional interaction with another living being, so the individual can let down human boundaries during the interaction.

Therapy dogs allow children to reveal their deepest thoughts and fears as well as be compassionate with another living being. Pet therapy also helps children in their separation from their pets at home. One little girl on our visit list was so upset from missing her pet at home. Maggie's warm and fuzzy hugs and her exchange of affection with this young lady appeared to lift her spirits and draw this patient's focus away from the inability to see her own pet.

Parents sometimes feel helpless and out of control when a child becomes ill and is hospitalized. When that toddler's mother I mentioned previously asked Maggie and I to visit, it gave her the ability to contribute a positive activity for her child. Pet therapy turns the antiseptic feel of a hospital unit into a more homelike setting.[7]

One child Maggie and I provided some therapy for was a nine-year-old, introverted girl who was extremely anxious and didn't trust anyone. She had been repeatedly sexually abused by her stepfather. She would hold Maggie's paw during the numerous procedures she underwent throughout her stay. I still remember her more relaxed demeanor and the broad smile plastered across her face when she and Maggie were together.

Children loved to see Maggie and I come and were always sad when we left. One seven-year-old kept repeating, "Just stay four more seconds, come on, just four more seconds." One little toddler absolutely

Joey and Maggie visit face to face

screamed when we left. He had not said a word during our visit, but he had seemed to enjoy being eye to eye with my compassionate, soft, and fuzzy friend.

Our pet visitations were considered by the nurses to be a non-conventional adjunct for pain control with the pediatric patients. One study that evaluated children ages five to eighteen found that canine visitation therapy "distracts children from pain-related cognition and possibly activates comforting thoughts regarding companionship and home."[8] Translation: dogs help children with their pain. Maggie certainly did, over and over again.

A most memorable pet visit with a child involved a road trip to Chicago. My cousin and her husband had a thirty-year-old son named Peter. With the cognitive capabilities of an eight-year-old and some autistic tendencies due to a brain tumor as an infant, Peter had required a lot of special attention growing up. My cousin Jane and her husband deserve much praise for their dedication and patience in raising Peter. Unfortunately, Peter had been in a go-cart accident recently and had suffered a severely displaced ankle fracture. He had been non-weight bearing for several weeks. When I called Jane to see what I could send Peter as a get-well surprise to occupy his time spent in a wheelchair, she said he loved dogs. I had learned about autistic behaviors that "being around household pets or having structured contact with animals can be a great addition to treatment."[9] The light came on. It was an ah-hah moment for sure! Why hadn't I thought of it earlier? Peter needed a therapy visit with Maggie.

It was our first long-distance, pet therapy house call. Maggie had a bubble bath, we packed every dog trick prop and Halloween costume in our repertoire, and away we went. Two hundred and fifty miles later, we were on Peter's doorstep. He knew me, but not very well, and he was timid. When I told him that my surprise was that I brought Maggie to see him, he replied, "I don't want to see her!"

I was prepared for his reaction. "Oh Peter, that's not the right answer," I responded and chuckled to myself. Finally, after some convincing, Peter was on board with Maggie coming into his home. Once Peter and Maggie became acquainted, she performed all her pet tricks and responded well to Peter's commands to do more. Maggie cooperated as Peter gave her some fairly vigorous pats and hugs. From time to time she and I would disappear, only to return with her modeling her different Halloween costumes.

The pet therapy visit for Peter was a memorable day for all of us. When my husband and I began our drive home, I was curious as to his perception of the afternoon. He had rarely been witness to what Maggie and I offer our patients. "I believe Peter enjoyed the visit very much," he said and then paused as he gathered his thoughts, "and wow, I think Maggie definitely deserves 'pet therapy dog of the day'!"

Maggie's Halloween costume entertains Peter

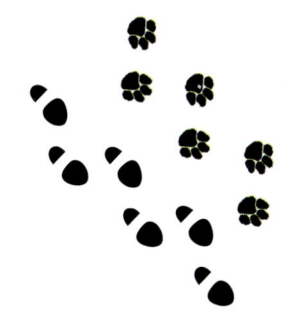

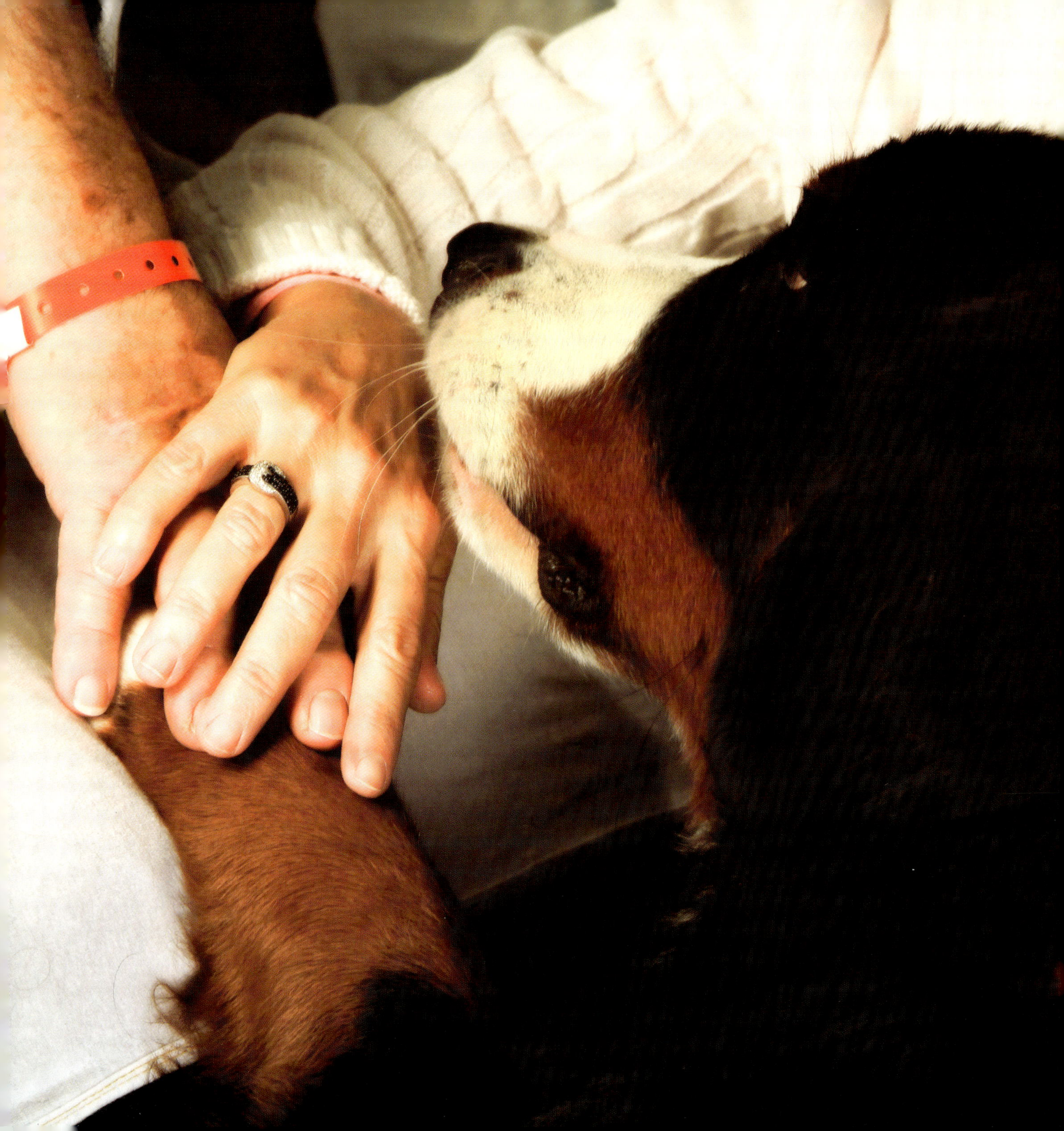

8
LAST ACT OF LOVE

It was a gorgeous Sunday afternoon, and I was just about to finish my weekend of two action-packed, 12-hour shifts. My role at the time was Nursing Supervisor, the person responsible for the flow of patient care throughout the hospital. After managing a heated patient and family dispute, responding to a deteriorating patient with emergent needs, and facilitating several new admissions, I was counting down the time until 6 p.m. when I would report off to the night shift supervisor.

Earlier in the weekend, I had been made aware that a co-worker's father was in his final hours of life. His family had decided against any resuscitative measures, and our nursing staff was providing what we call "comfort measures only." So it should not have surprised me to have Mary, my friend, stop me in the hall to give me another update on her dad's condition. What I wasn't expecting was her request that I bring Maggie in to see him. Many thoughts ran through my head as I probably hesitated in my response. When did she want us to come? It had to be right after work that day, since there was a good chance he would pass on in the next several hours. Didn't she realize I'd been here all weekend already? Of what benefit would Maggie and I be in this grave and grieving atmosphere? I selfishly came up with an excuse.

"Gosh, Mary. Maggie isn't freshly bathed, since I've been working all weekend."

"That doesn't matter," she said quickly. "You know what we're going through, and we could all use a little cheering up."

I agreed to come. I called my daughter to see if she could meet me at the hospital front door with Maggie as soon as my shift ended.

I often had told Andrea, my 25-year-old daughter, that Maggie knew when she was going to work. She would start barking with excitement when I would pull up at the hospital with her. Andrea wasn't used to handling my ninety-seven pound Bernese Mountain Dog, and she was certainly not expecting Maggie's reaction as she opened her car door that day. My normally well-mannered dog jumped over Andrea's lap, shoved her way out of the car, and ran to greet me at the hospital front door. Andrea was not happy.

"Geez, your dog is out of control!" she said.

I just smiled and replied, "I told you she gets wound up on her way to do pet therapy." I'm pretty sure Andrea believed me after that incident.

I was talking to Maggie (and probably preparing myself too) as we entered the elevator. "Maggie, we have a special visit to make today, and you have to be on your best behavior. This patient is really sick, and his family is very sad."

As we approached the patient's room, I noticed there were many family members of all ages present. It was difficult for Maggie and me just to maneuver our way to the bedside. The lights were dim, and we felt a solemn demeanor amidst the well wishers, several of whom had teary eyes. My friend Mary spotted us immediately and asked that we come closer to her dad's bed.

"Daddy," Mary said softly, "I have a surprise for you. My friend brought Maggie, our therapy dog, to see you. Maggie makes everyone around here feel better." His eyes were closed, but Mary took her dad's hand. Together they gently stroked Maggie. "Isn't she soft?" Mary said to her dad. As I knew she would, Maggie didn't move a muscle, and her big, brown eyes remained fixed on Mary's dad. Mary's dad never opened his eyes, but he briefly nodded his head in affirmation.

Mary removed her hand. Slowly her dad started petting Maggie on his own. It was a very emotional moment. Everyone in the room was moved by the caring interaction. Mary's mom then intervened with her own request. "Maggie, you look like a fluffy teddy bear, and Lord only knows I need a big hug about now." I encouraged Maggie to take a few steps so that Mary's mom could reach her. Again, another stretch of silence as Mary's mom embraced my furry friend.

The stillness was broken when Mary asked if we could show her children and their cousins some of Maggie's tricks. She cleared a space in the middle of the room, and we went to work. The serious tone quickly turned to one of giggles and "aaaaw, that's so cute!" More of Mary's family came into the room, so at Mary's request, we repeated Maggie's repertoire of tricks.

After about thirty minutes, Mary saw us to the door and thanked us for our visit. As I walked to the car, I thought of the difficult time Mary's family was experiencing. I wondered how I could have been so self-centered initially to consider not honoring her request.

I now know exactly why Mary had wanted Maggie and me to visit her father when his death was eminent. I realize that the benefit of pet therapy in this grave situation was for my calming pet therapy dog to provide comfort, understanding, and love to Mary and her family. As one author states, the benefit of dogs visiting patients at such a critical time is that "their presence is an oasis of beauty and serenity."[1]

Hopefully my heart experienced some growth. From that day forward, I had a greater respect for those who requested us, and for Maggie's ability to touch humans even amidst the most grave of care settings, impending death.

I saw Mary about a week later and expressed my sympathy for the loss of her father. She thanked me profusely for our visit. She said something I'll never forget. "That was the last act of love I was able to do for my father. I will be forever grateful."

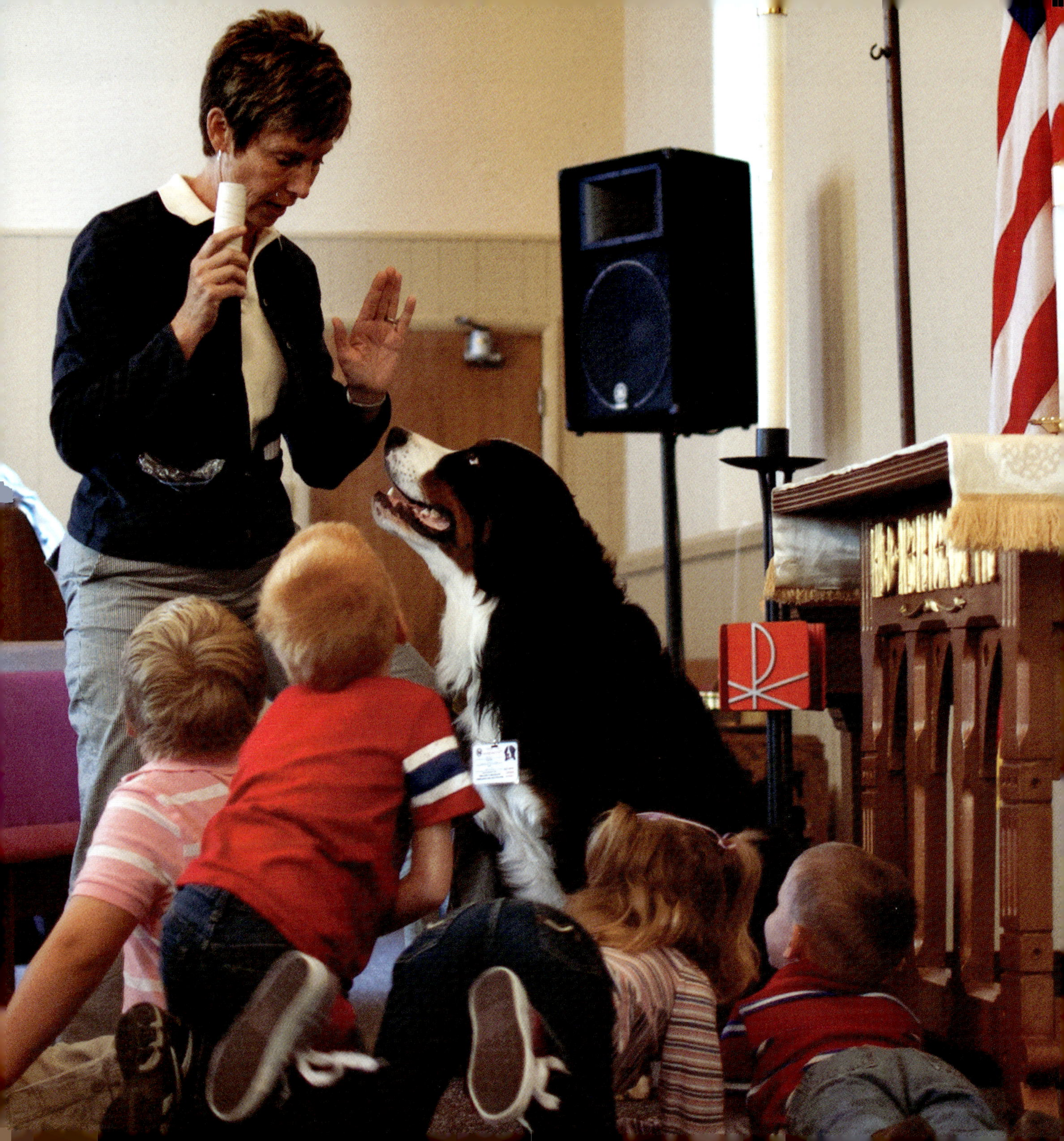

9
A SPIRITUAL CONNECTION

I was supposed to be totally focused on the children's sermon message that day in church. Instead, I was distracted by the restlessness of several youngsters gathered around the minister as he tried hard to make a biblical point amidst their squirming antics. I had another "ah-hah" moment. If I could bring Maggie into the sanctuary, perhaps we would lure the attention of our little people by having a live dog in church. I was envisioning an audience of captive listeners.

Before I approached others in our congregation with my idea, I questioned the appropriateness of this "new to our church" canine ministry. The rationale I found was not complicated. The Bible talks about animals numerous times. The story of Noah's ark describes God requesting Noah to "bring in the animals, too—a pair of each" onto the ark (Genesis 7:2 Life Application Bible).[1] The Bible also describes several times when animals walked side by side with man.

My conclusion was that animals are one of God's many gifts, and He had given me this beautiful creature not only to enrich the lives of others, but also to spread His Word. I found this verse: "Is there any such thing as Christians cheering each other up?" (Philippians 2:1).[2] The Bible also says that we can learn spiritual lessons from animals. "Ask the dumbest beast—he knows that it is so; ask the birds—they will tell you … For the soul of every living thing is in the hand of God" (Job 12:7-10).[3]

A SPIRITUAL CONNECTION

After deciding that this concept was not only appropriate but also supported by Scripture, I ran my idea past some Sunday school teachers and our minister. I was granted the green light, and before long Maggie and I were preparing a message for the children. Children's sermons and spiritual healing soon became another phase of our journey.

We had a great turnout for Maggie's first mini message. Not only did the children come up to the front of the church, but also they gathered intimately around us. One toddler, perhaps thinking Maggie was a stuffed animal, listened for a while from atop her back. I thought Maggie and I had these little people focused on the elementary point we were making of being kind to everyone. Then Maggie made a big yawn, and a little boy said, "Wow, does she have a big mouth!" That innocent assessment of my furry theological assistant led everyone in the congregation temporarily astray from our message at hand!

The message that day on kindness to others seemed especially appropriate, as it's also one that Maggie had demonstrated often in our nursing home visits. We focused on being kind to all and not being judgmental. "In this new life, one's nationality or race or education is unimportant. Whether a person has Christ is what matters. Because of His deep love for you, practice tenderhearted mercy and kindness to others" (Colossians 3:11-12).[4]

Our children's message

In subsequent children's messages, I incorporated pet tricks that drove home certain concepts. For instance, I demonstrated how Maggie stared at me while heeling at my side as an example of always watching

God as we go through life. When cued, Maggie would nod her head as if to agree with a point I was trying to make. She would retrieve a scrolled document from her "purse" that contained the Bible verse. The messages always ended with Maggie lying across her little red stool and bowing her head when I prayed.

Maggie and I have been given the opportunity to provide several messages to the children of my church and other Christian youth settings. I would highly recommend this medium as an effective way of spreading God's Word. One researcher writes of the possible spiritual connection of animals and suggests that they "catalyze a spiritual component of healing." That researcher then explains, "There is in every animal's eye a dim image and a gleam of humanity, a flash of strange light, through which their life looks at and up to our great mystery of command over them, and claims the fellowship of the creature, if not of the soul."[5]

hat Looks Right?
Words With Two or
ore Patterns
Brand Name Phonics
Learning One- and Two-Syllable Words that Follow a Pattern, but Are Used Less Frequently
Dictionary
What Happens On Spring Break
STAYS
On Spring Break!
AEROPOSTALE
I'm Gonna Like Me

10
EXPANDING OUR SCOPE

Maggie and I had been visiting patients for over a year, and creative requests for our services continued to come. Inpatient and outpatient service lines, non-clinical departments, and community groups were contacting us. Although these invitations weren't all geared toward the most common kinds of patient population of the hospital, they all supported one common thread, the therapeutic, human-animal relationship.

It made sense to me that the human-animal relationship could be of assistance in a broad spectrum of settings. It can be experienced by many people, is often deep and sometimes everlasting, and relaxes personal boundaries. According to Dr. Larry Dossey, holistic physician, the bond that forms may be described as an unconditional connection and positive feeling between an animal and a human where there is relaxing of personal boundaries, a mutual trust, and a willingness to let down one's guard and act naturally.[1] I was intrigued to discover

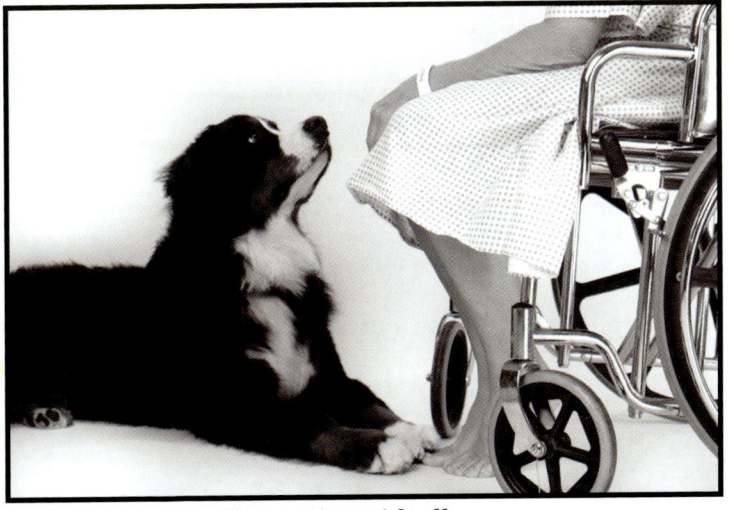

Connecting with all ages

the effects my huggable health care partner was having on people in our widening spectrum of settings.

As Maggie and I approached the medical inpatient unit one day, we couldn't help but hear the intermittent yelling of a patient suffering from dementia. Amidst her daunting outbursts were words of encouragement as her nurse attempted to persuade her to take her pills. We tried quietly to bypass that room, but the nurse spotted us and motioned for our assistance. "Maybe Maggie can help," she said. "Nothing else works." It wasn't the first time we had the opportunity to connect with a very confused geriatric patient, but it was definitely a reminder of the temporary change in behavior that can occur with pet therapy intervention. The frenzied cries of this woman stopped as she stared at my dog. I encouraged Maggie to rest her head on the patient's bed, diverting the patient's focus to her newfound friend. As she focused on Maggie, she opened her mouth and swallowed her mashed up medication in applesauce.

One researcher explains that pet therapy can "effectively address several of the diminished life skills resulting from dementia."[2] For example, withdrawal can be less due to stimulation of the patient's senses. Short- and long-term memory can be enhanced, as well as communication skills.[3] Here, once again, Maggie was able to experience what research has shown, the simple yet effective outcomes of animal-human interaction. The nurses were the ones that gave Maggie a hug that day.

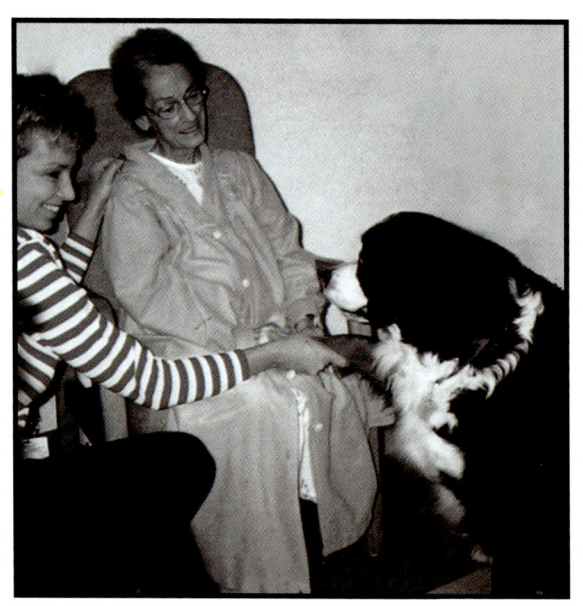

Maggie offers her paw

Maggie and I began to develop close relationships with some of our recurring patients. For example, a lovely lady in her seventies named Patsy had a heart valve disease that brought her to the hospital frequently. I had the opportunity to assist in her care in my nursing supervisor role. Whenever she was in our hospital as an inpatient, Maggie and I would visit her. Although Patsy was burdened by ill health, she always greeted us with a smile. She and I would share stories about our pets and families. Both Maggie and I grew close to Patsy and her very dedicated husband. At Patsy's funeral, Harry, her husband, thanked Maggie and I for being "angels in Patsy's life" and for bringing joy and encouragement through her chronic health battles.

Patients with cardiac related illnesses were one of the frequent focuses of our pet therapy visits, since this specific population could benefit in multiple ways. One researcher wrote of the outcomes that occurred following a 12-minute interaction with a pet therapy team. Improved heart and lung pressures, hormone levels, and anxiety were documented in patients hospitalized with heart failure.[4]

Our first outpatient request came from the physical rehabilitation department. An eight-year-old boy with a history of physical abuse needed some outpatient, goal-directed therapy. He had difficulty interacting with his family and refused to carry out tasks that had been assigned to him. His mother described him as a "behavioral nightmare." The director of the department contacted me with the idea of using Maggie as a motivational tool for Jimmy. Research has documented that children view animals as peers and can interact with them better than they can with people.[5]

The physical therapist told little Jimmy that Maggie was brought in solely to have fun with him. She informed us that Jimmy was challenged in following directions, such as completing a task. The little guy seemed full of non-focused energy, but we were pleasantly surprised that he kept his attention on Maggie. Karen, the therapist, was quite clever in her goal-directed activities. Jimmy and Maggie played catch with toys, climbed up and down the rehab stairs, and moved to specified destinations in the large room. For the first time since Maggie and I had been working as a team, I took on a different role, that of strictly an observer. Maggie was a bit confused by the change in process. At one point when Jimmy jogged by me with Maggie on her leash, she appeared out of breath with this burst of physical exertion. My four-legged, pampered princess gazed at me as if to say, *What's with this exercise stuff?*

Our next outpatient assignment was much less strenuous, as we were asked to participate in a speech therapy session with a four-year-old cerebral palsy patient. Shawna was just learning to talk but needed lots of encouragement. So once again, Maggie filled the role of motivator in improving this specific skill. Through simple interactions between the therapist, Shawna, and Maggie, Shawna was able to speak these words slowly and softly: dog, toy, brush, paws, and dog treats. During the interactions, Maggie lay on the floor next to Shawna and seemed gently respectful of her legs in braces. Eventually the therapist had Shawna giving Maggie commands, and Maggie responded with a display of her silly dog tricks.

The advances we witnessed with Shawna support the theory that communication skills can be enhanced through conversation using animals.[6] Speech impaired patients can improve their own vocalization by verbalizing to a dog, identifying its body parts, or saying commands that are clear enough for the dog to understand.[7] The rewarding piece of this experience came from Shawna's mother, who sat on the other side of a mirror/observation window. I was humbled to hear her tearful enthusiasm over Shawna's progress.

Through these and many other experiences in animal assisted therapy, I realized that what might seem to others as trivial rehabilitation accomplishments were welcome progress. One researcher has stated that the "unconditional love of dogs helps lift the spirits of patients and encourages them to persevere in therapy."[8] Improved coordination, balance, and muscle strength are examples of outcomes from a simple game of fetch with a dog in the rehabilitation world.[9]

As Maggie and I continued to expand our scope, I found out that pet therapy could be used to close the gap in challenging interpersonal relationships. For example, we had one patient named Judy who had some ongoing health concerns that caused chronic pain. Judy was addicted to her pain medications and would become quite testy with nursing staff and supervisors when she made demands that were not in her best interest. Nurses did not deviate from physician orders, but Judy's persistence created a frustrating, fatiguing environment for staff. Maggie had a calming effect on her that led her to refocus her disruptive behavior in a positive direction. Pet therapy seemed to create an emotionally safe, non-threatening tone that soothed Judy's anxious demeanor.

I also discovered great value in the health care team's awareness of the role that therapy dogs could have in promoting holistic health. We, as nurses, have multiple types of therapeutic opportunities at our disposal. "As patient advocates, if we believe that a visit from an animal therapist … may benefit the patient's physiological and emotional well-being, then we should strive to safely incorporate such visits into the plan of care."[10] Because of Maggie's positive results, this complimentary, cost-effective means of supporting mental, physical, and social recovery became more favorably considered.

One author stated, "It is justified to accept that those people who interact with pet animals may benefit from improved physical, psychological and social health experiences and animals can also provide specific benefits for special groups in society."[11] The nursing staff and hospital staff as a whole began to embrace the positive attributes of Maggie's presence and realize that pet therapy also offered an uplifting and empathetic gesture of kindness.

One example of staff considering pet therapy as an avenue of healing involved one of the hospital's employees who became extremely ill. He was loved and respected by those with whom he worked. His peers knew he and his wife were dog lovers, and as a gesture of concern, suggested Maggie and I pay him an inpatient visit. We actually saw him on more than one occasion. Apparently Maggie's presence was impactful, as his staff also encouraged Maggie and me to attend his retirement party.

Holiday visits to patients were added to our scope. Maggie rounded in her Halloween costume on Halloween and was encouraged by nurses to stop in to see their specific patients. She also was invited to participate in the annual employee Christmas party. She was even asked to sit right next to Santa. My husband remarked, as Maggie left our house on the morning of the party with jingle bell collar and Santa hat in place, "Maggie, one word of advice. Don't steal Santa's thunder."

Our mission was to compliment Santa's presence and honor the request of over two hundred children for a picture with Maggie. There were several small children who were afraid to have their pictures taken with Santa, so Maggie became their other option. One memorable comment came from a five-year-old little boy after his photo had been taken with Maggie. "Daddy, I didn't know that Santa had a dog named Maggie."

Maggie at the employee Christmas party

In 2007 the nursing staff asked us to partner with them in their efforts to achieve Magnet status, the highest national recognition awarded to outstanding nursing programs. Maggie was to pull a cart of baked goods around the hospital to raise funds for the application expenses. That task in itself required some education. Bernese Mountain Dogs are typically timid, and it took a good month of diligent training for Maggie to comfortably and effectively perform carting. The nurses were appreciative of our efforts, as they sold lots of donated goods. It was fun, but the logistics of maneuvering a large dog and cart around tight corners and backing in and out of elevators weren't ones we wanted to partake in very often.

Well deserved staff pet therapy

I'd been reading about a new, non-health care concept in which dogs assist school children with reading deficits by having the children "read to the dog." Surrounding scholastically challenged youngsters with their peers can lead to embarrassment, loss of self-esteem, and loss of desire to practice reading. This new program, instead, suggested positioning a dog with a child in a secluded area. The environment would then become for the child relaxing, non-intimidating, positive, fun, and effective. One successful program called R.E.A.D. (Reading Education Assistance Dogs) explains that literacy skills can be enhanced by incorporating certified therapy teams as reading mentors.[12]

Expanding Our Scope

Miss Angie, a friend of our family who taught fourth grade, had a classroom of eager candidates for our first experience in reading with Maggie. First Angie had Maggie sit in the middle of each reading group as they started their story. She then asked the children to take turns spending time in an isolated area with just Maggie and me. Knowing that this type of therapy would require my canine partner to be very quiet and calm, I made sure we took a long walk. One morning, perhaps, it turned out to be too long of a walk. During the reading experience with an adorable little blonde, curly haired boy with thick glasses named Daniel, I could tell Maggie was getting sleepy. Daniel noticed Maggie's slowly fading attention to his story reading, and he asked me, "Mrs. Myers, why are Maggie's eyes closing?"

"Because she is concentrating on every word you are saying," I replied.

He then asked me, "Mrs. Myers, why is Maggie snoring?"

I was stumped and had no response, but I did give Maggie a hidden nudge to disturb her deep sleep.

These and many other scenarios of pet therapy exemplify the broad spectrum of opportunities that exist for pet therapy teams in and outside of the hospital setting. As Maggie and I did, pet therapy teams can collaborate with many different disciplines to plan individual approaches, depending on the behavioral and functional needs. Maggie and I grew from each experience as we attempted to offer healing moments of care.

The Visit

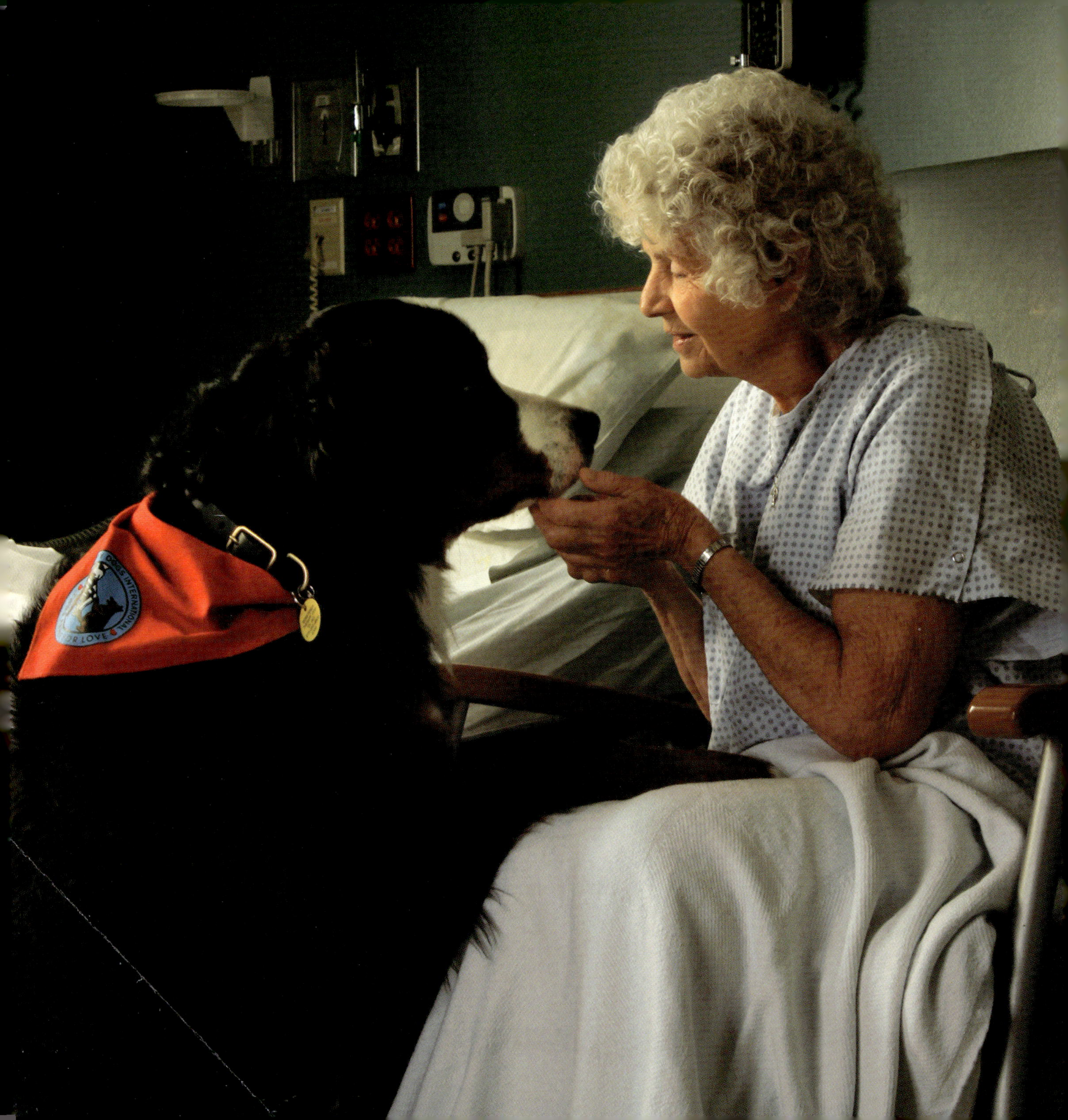
DOGS INTERNATIONAL

11
EMBRACING THE ELDERLY

The first time I accompanied my four-footed therapist to our local nursing home for an exploratory round of visits, I didn't know if Maggie would show interest in the patients, or if they would express any desire to visit us. So when Connie, the activities director, offered to introduce us to the residents who might enjoy pet therapy, we were most appreciative.

I think back and chuckle at that first comment we heard from a resident. Maggie and I noticed an aged, frail lady who expressed little emotion and was seated in an awkward position in her worn recliner. She seemed to come alive as we drew near to her. All of the sudden, she pointed at Maggie, held her nose, and shouted, "Pee-uww! Get that stinky dog out of here." I looked at Connie with a raised brow and thought, *Are you sure this is going to work?*

We moved on to a group of men sitting in a semicircle around the television. One of them leaned forward over the tray of his geriatric chair, which we accepted as a gesture of interest. We slowly approached him, and when we were within reach, he started petting Maggie. Just as I noticed that he was large in stature, he grabbed hold of Maggie's leash firmly and wouldn't let go. She froze in place except for her eyes, which looked back and forth between him and me. I petted her and assured her, "It's okay, girl." I kindly took control of her leash and started telling the resident all about Maggie and why we were visiting. He seemed "pleasantly confused" (as we nurses refer to kind and friendly individuals suffering from dementia), but my words brought a meek smile of understanding on his face. Once I felt Maggie was relaxed, I asked her to put her paws on the arm of his wheelchair. Our visit with John ended on a positive note for Maggie, as she was the recipient of a vigorous back rub.

We followed Connie to the next wing of the facility, where she explained that patients there required a higher level of care. Again, we observed several patients in a semicircle. Connie introduced us to most of them. They appeared to be wheelchair bound, so we made our way around the group, one person at a time, to share the experience of petting Maggie. One sweet lady named Milly was quite talkative and told me all about her former lap dog. Her face warmed up and her demeanor softened as she elaborated about her old fuzzy friend. As she shared those pleasant memories, I recalled reading that the number one thing that geriatric patients find difficulty parting with when entering a nursing home is a pet.[1] Since I was a huge animal lover, this fact made perfect sense to me. Why should these individuals be deprived of touching warm and fuzzy creatures like my Maggie, who can provide much comfort? I made a mental note that every time we came to that facility, we would make an effort for Maggie to visit Milly.

As we had just about completed our "meet and greet" with everyone in the semicircle, I noticed Maggie was staring at a man positioned in the corner of the room. I looked at Connie, and she volunteered to tell us about Arnold. She said she thought he would love to see Maggie because he was a huge dog lover. He even slept with a stuffed dog in his bed. This man had very limited use of his arms, so he was reclined, awkwardly so it seemed, in a geriatric chair. I said hello to Arnold, told him my name, and said my big dog had come to see him. He grinned from ear to ear. I then gave Maggie the command to place her paws on the arms of his wheelchair so he could get a good look at her. She gently wagged her tail, tuned into his facial expressions, and didn't seem to notice or take offense to his unshaven face or toothless, drooling smile and inability to pet her.

Eventually Maggie's attention was drawn to some crumbs on the towel that acted as a bib on Arthur's chest. Positioned only inches from those morsels of food, Maggie looked at me, at the crumbs, and then back at me. God bless her. Although she was doing such a good job as a fairly new therapy dog for geriatric patients and had accepted this man regardless of his afflictions, she was still an animal who loved food. I said, "No, Maggie, not a good idea," and I asked her to get down.

I noticed it was approaching 3 p.m., so I told Connie we had time to go to one more area. I tried to be observant of my surroundings so I could navigate independently on our next visit. Maggie noticed this individual before I did. The tension on her leash alerted me, and Maggie led me to a woman in a wheelchair. On her own, my dog positioned herself directly in front of this neatly kept lady. Not a word was spoken, but both of their facial expressions spoke volumes, and their connection seemed to be immediate. Connie and I observed Maggie's reassuring way of interrupting this resident's loneliness. I was fortunate to capture that spontaneous, non-verbal encounter on my camera. What a great demonstration it was of the nurturing ability of these four-legged therapists to focus in on those in need.

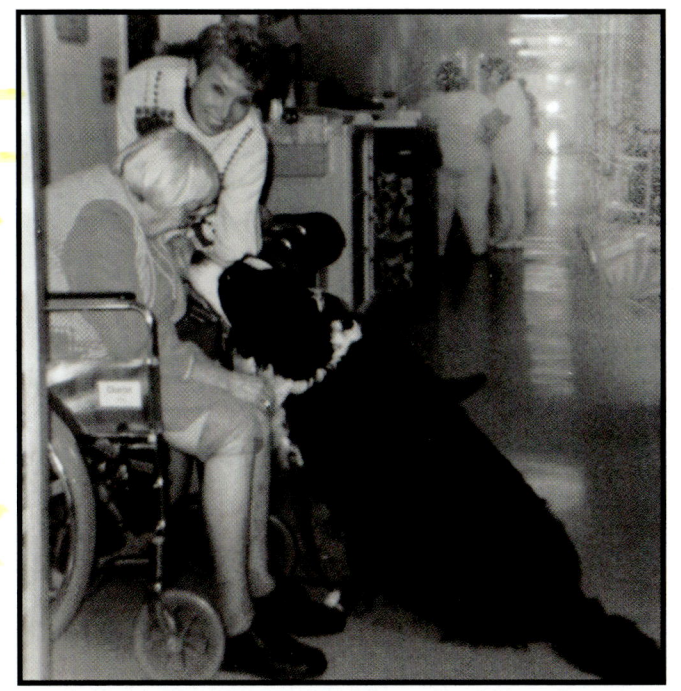

An in-depth conversation without words

For our last encounter, Connie turned into a small alcove where a very plain, somewhat alert but withdrawn lady in her fifties lay partially reclined in her wheelchair. Connie leaned over to speak directly to Martha. "Hey, sleepyhead, wake up. You have a surprise visitor today."

Connie motioned Maggie to come closer. I was so glad my dog had been schooled on how to put her paws on the arms of a wheelchair, a move that had come in handy multiple times already at this facility. I cued her to assume that position one last time. Martha's eyes got as big as saucers. (When I relived this story to my husband that night, he said, "Wouldn't your eyes get as big as saucers too if a hundred-pound dog suddenly appeared at your chest?") I introduced us and told Martha a little about Maggie and why we were visiting her. She seemed to stare holes through us. Eventually her facial expression began to soften, and she calmly, slowly, and distinctly said, "My, you are a beautiful dog. Thank you for visiting me."

My attention was diverted suddenly from these simple but gratifying words of kindness to the commotion at the nurses' station. It was shift change time, so several staff members were present. I looked around the room to see what they were "oohing and aahing" about but noticed nothing out of the ordinary. I looked back at the nurses' station and saw then that most of them had their eyes on Martha and Maggie. One of the nurses explained, "Martha hasn't spoken in months."

At that moment, no one else uttered a word. It took a second for the nurse's comment to sink in to me. Wow. Maggie had done nothing out of the ordinary, yet all of us in the room that day had just witnessed a heart-warming, verbal response from Martha.

Research supports the fact that a unique and humanlike relationship can occur between animals and humans and result in unexplainable responses. "The mere presence of a dog may facilitate interactions with the non-communicative patient."[2] I am still in awe and humbled that Maggie's brief encounter with Martha would motivate her to speak. It was definitely a healing moment!

We had stayed at the nursing home much longer than planned. As we briskly headed back through the halls, we heard the same voice that had first greeted us when we arrived. "Hey, lady, bring that dog over here. I want to pet her." What an about-face this resident had made. Maggie and I immediately changed our course and went over to visit the lady who earlier had shouted that Maggie smelled bad. Though we were running late, we didn't want to rob this resident of the opportunity to interact with my compassionate, fluffy friend. What a great way to end our visit.

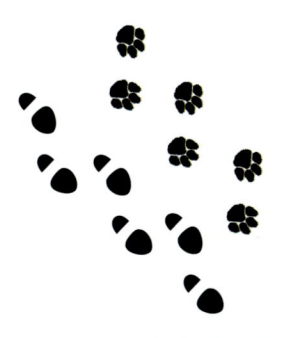

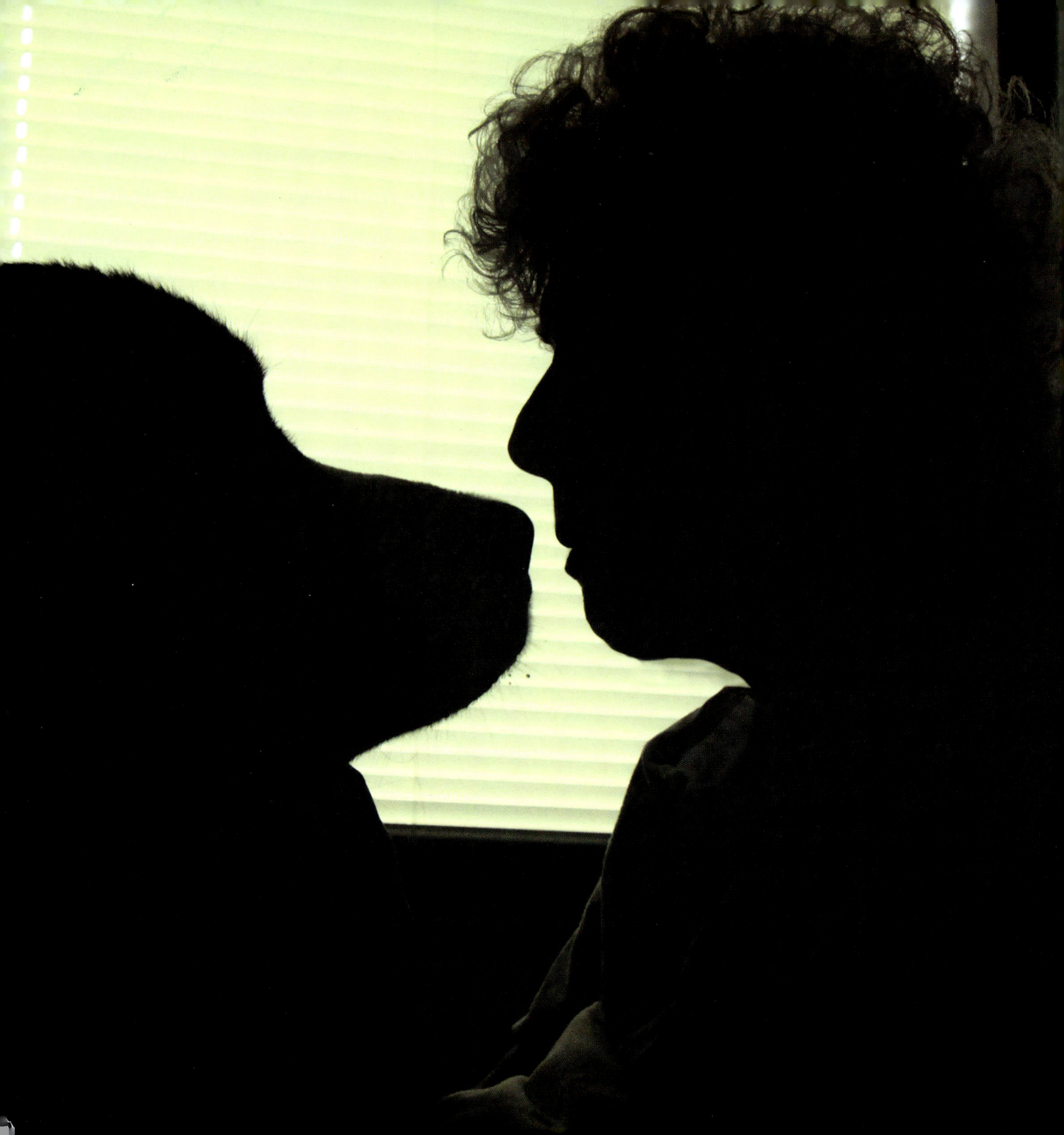

12
LOST VISION, GAINED INSIGHT

Critical care patients are often deprived of the simple joys in life due to the physiological crises that have engulfed their world.[1] The severity of their illnesses necessitates a priority focus on intense medical management. In the meantime, their comfortable, normal living environments at home are replaced by more sterile, less relaxing settings punctuated by beeping medical equipment. These patients temporarily cease living with their loved ones and pets, which compromises their personal network of emotional support.

My multiple years as a bedside nurse who observed the critical care patient experience had instilled in me a burning desire to offer pet therapy is this setting. Pet visits "reduce stress" and "normalize the hospital environment", creating a more homelike atmosphere.[2] Therapy dogs' ability to reduce loneliness, encourage staff and family interaction, build trust, and lower anxiety qualify them as an appropriate, complimentary therapy for the critical patient plan of care. Pet therapy dogs also offer a variety of "unique and humanistic therapeutic interventions"[3] for critical care patients. These animals can provide stimulus for comatose patients, assist in orienting confused patients to reality, improve patients' body image, and reduce the need for medication. As the health of critical care patients improves, pet therapy can provide motivation during rehabilitation and act as an incentive for patients to resume life with their families (and pets, if they have them).[4]

It takes a special dog to administer pet therapy to the critical care patient. The dog's temperament must be "bomb proof" to the high levels of stimulus, noises, and commotion. The dog can't be easily distracted by the multiple tubes and machines that might surround these patients or the stressful behaviors exhibited by patients or family members.[5] Maggie had demonstrated consistently calm and patient focused behaviors while visiting patients on the other medical floors, and I felt she was ready for the challenge of interacting with intensive care level patients.

At this point in our pet therapy experience, the hospital staff in general was not only "tolerating" (as that former Risk Manager had put it) but also embracing and encouraging our mission. The timing was right to approach the Director of Intensive Care to discuss how visits from Maggie and me could be of value to her specific patient population. After receiving her support, we began to include the Intensive Care Unit in our regular pet therapy rounds.

As Maggie and I were heading toward ICU one afternoon, a distinguished older gentleman approached us. "Is this the pet therapy dog I've been hearing about? If so, I'd like for you to pay my wife a visit. I can't guarantee she'll let you in, but can you at least try?"

This man seemed very concerned and was looking for someone, anyone, to reach out to his wife. We peeked into ICU Room Six, and there sat a very attractive and well-kept lady in her seventies. She was slumped over in her wheelchair and appeared to be staring at the walls, not seeming to care about anything. When I respectfully knocked on her door and told her who we were, she assumed a more attentive position and said with a tone of authority in her voice, "Bring your dog over here where I can pet her."

I led Maggie up to Mrs. Corne and stepped back to confer with her husband. He explained that his wife had recently experienced a serious cerebral bleed that had caused her to loose her vision. Her reaction was one of anger and disbelief, as she was a doctorate prepared educator and not used to idle time. With this new knowledge of the patient's visual deficit, I approached Maggie, took hold of Mrs. Corne's outreached hand, and placed it on my dog, who had assumed a position right in front of the patient.

"Maggie, I'm nothing to look at, am I? I can't see a damn thing, and I hate it," stated Mrs. Corne. She then proceeded to dialogue solely with Maggie, telling her all about the onset of her illness and her concern that her vision might not return. Mrs. Corne rambled on for quite some time, pausing when she was overcome with emotion. The piece that Maggie gave to the conversation was her undivided attention and good listening ears.

After some time, there was a stretch of silence. Mr. Corne and I watched his wife carefully run her fingers over and over Maggie's body. She then made a comment directly to me. "What a nice dog. I don't know much about these Bernese Mountain Dogs, but I imagine they're related to Saint Bernards. I used to raise Saints, and I even did a little pet therapy myself. It works, you know." At that point Mr. Corne winked at me, as he felt his plan was being well received.

"Your dog has lovely markings. I bet you're proud of her," she continued. I couldn't imagine how she knew what Maggie's markings were, since she was blind. I'm glad she followed with an explanation, because I wasn't about to ask. "There's a difference in texture between her more coarse, black hair and her silky, white strands. Haven't you noticed that?"

I felt a bit negligent as Maggie's partner not to have known that, but I was thrilled to see that this first, uncomplicated visit with Mrs. Corne had brought some much needed pleasure to her upside down world.

Another patient that we frequently saw in ICU was Mrs. Schmidt. She was a larger framed, very vivacious lady with a strong German accent. She unfortunately had end-stage congestive heart failure, which necessitated frequent trips to ICU. One day when we came for a visit, the nurses, who had grown to be great supporters of our mission, relayed the story of Mrs. Schmidt's 1 a.m. admission that morning. They had worked feverishly to stabilize her respiratory status. Finally by about 5 a.m., she was responding to her newly started medications. She was breathing easier, her oxygen saturations had improved, and she was exhibiting compliance in leaving her oxygen mask in place. At that time, one of the attending nurses said, "Mrs. Schmidt, it's almost morning, and you've not gotten hardly any sleep. Is there anything else we can do for you before we leave your room?"

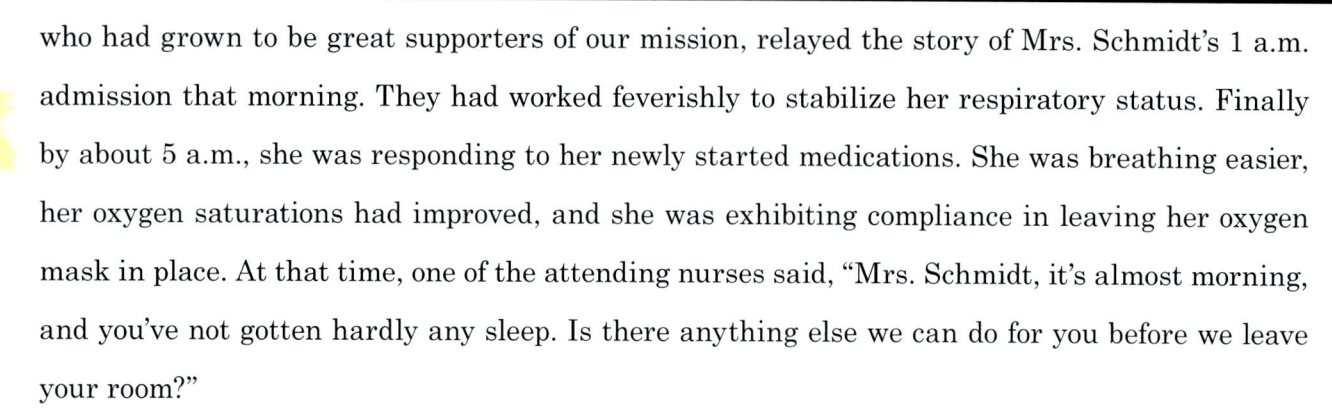

Without hesitation the patient responded, "Yes, I want to know when that big black dog is going to visit me again." First things first, even at five o'clock in the morning!

The Visit

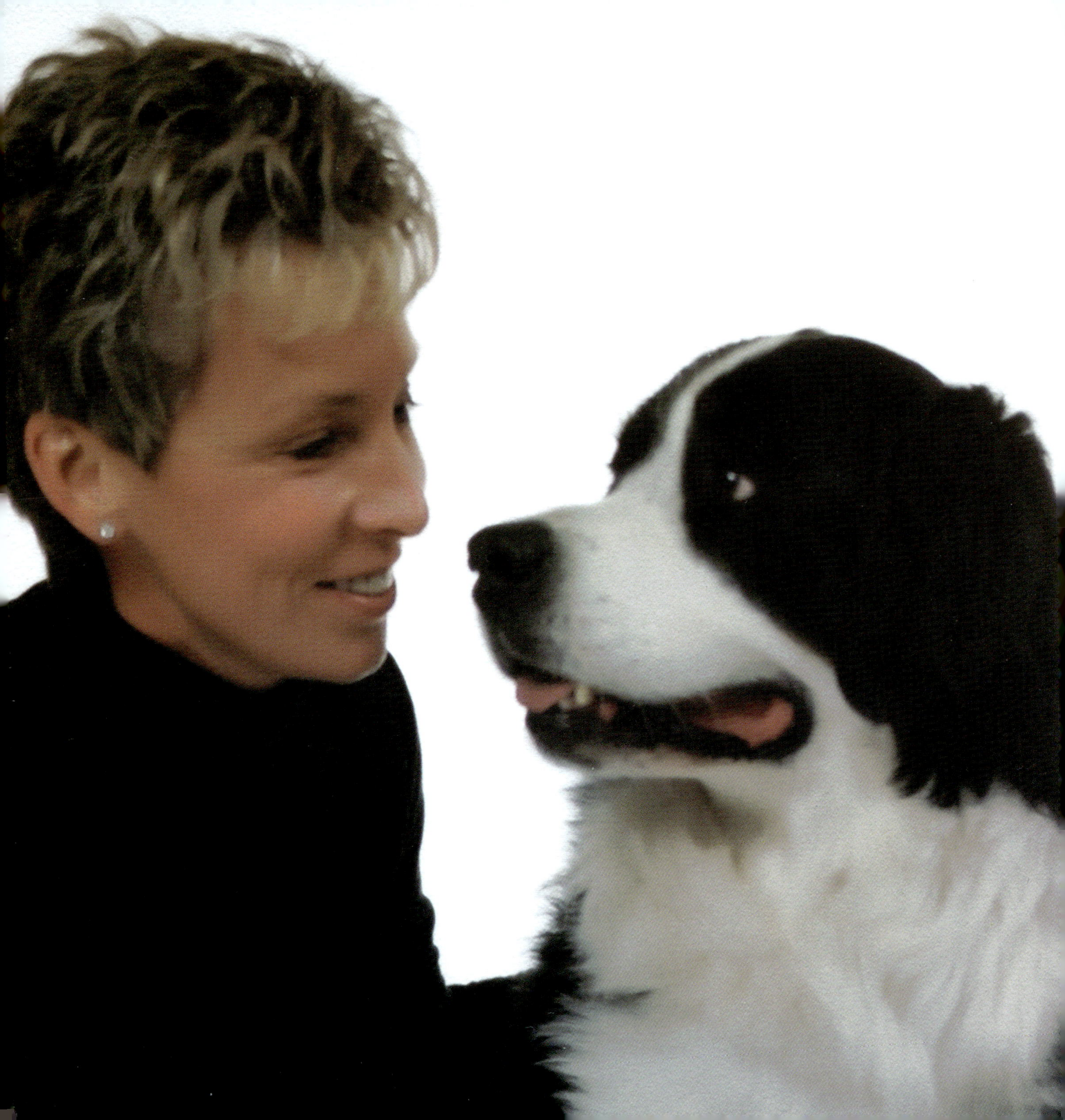

13
MY DEFENDER

It was nine degrees outside at 8 a.m. that February Saturday morning. I had already fed the horses, cleaned the stalls, and was ready for a walk with the dogs. After a full week at my hospital job, I was looking forward to getting back outside on the weekend. I headed across the dam and through the field with Maggie and also Duke and Jack, my son's two Labradors. We stopped by my daughter Andrea's house to invite her and her Jack Russell to come along.

As I stood on her front porch, I commented how beautiful it was outside with the snowflakes falling. We had awakened to a fresh dusting of snow. Andrea, not an early riser, seemed unimpressed and uninterested in joining us. She did suggest that I be careful, as there were some frozen puddles from the huge rain we'd received earlier in the week. And she gave permission for her high-energy Jack Russell to accompany us. She watched as he cleared the edge of the porch to catch up with the other dogs.

About two hundred yards later, we were all enjoying the day. The dogs were acting crazed to be outdoors and running free in the crisp, morning chill. My gait fluctuated between a slow jog and a brisk walk. We were on a walking path between the edge of the woods and the harvested bean field when all of the sudden, I slid on a big patch of ice that was hidden by a thin layer of snow. My ankle turned under me, and I sat on it forcefully with my entire body weight. As I lay back to assess my injuries, my leg felt immediately numb. Leaning on my elbows, legs straight out in front of me, I noticed my one foot was facing the wrong way. Oh, my gosh! It didn't take being a nurse to figure out that I had just suffered an extremely displaced fracture.

The next thing I remember was dogs barking everywhere. The two Labs and the Jack Russell were circling, probably thinking I was on the ground to play. The frigid temperature seemed to heighten their energy level. I was so afraid they were going to run across my distorted ankle. But Maggie could sense otherwise. She came and stood calmly, right by my face, looking over me. Then she started showing her teeth to those other dogs, taking on a killer attitude. Where did that behavior come from? I'd never seen it in her. She appeared to be responding to my condition in some instinctual and aggressive defense mode, a trait I didn't know even existed in my gentle companion. Next, to my amazement, Maggie stepped across my chest, straddled my belly, and ever so carefully lowered herself on top of me. Because it was only nine degrees outside and I was resting on a sheet of ice, her warm, furry body brought me comfort as I considered what to do about my situation.

My daughter's friend had just driven into the driveway. As he stepped out of his car, he noticed me lying out in the field. He immediately told my daughter. She looked out the window briefly, but the dogs and I were quite far from the house. "Oh, she's fine," she told her friend. "It looks like she's making snow angels with the dogs."

Fortunately I had my cell phone with me, so I placed a call for help to Andrea and to my husband. My exact words (so they tell me) were, "I am absolutely positively sure I broke something. Come get me."

When help arrived, Maggie was reluctant, first of all, to get off of me and second, to get in one vehicle without me after she observed me getting into another. My daughter helped me stabilize my leg before I could be transferred into her truck. (Only a nurse and dog lover would stabilize her own fracture by strapping her extremity to a two-by-four piece of wood with a dog leash. And only a nurse would call ahead to the emergency room and tell the staff to get ready for her arrival—pain medication included.)

The technical term for my ankle injury was a "comminuted bi-malleolar fracture with obvious deformity." I was transferred to another hospital, where I was taken right to surgery. I'm still sporting several screws and a couple of steel plates, but thankfully I was eventually able to resume all physical activity, including running.

I had always wondered if Maggie would protect me if the need arose. One researcher states, "The extent to which animals respond to humans in need is simply stunning. They often appear to invoke ways of knowing that defy explanation … not only do animals care for humans, they often appear to grieve when they are separated from the humans they love."[1] There's no doubt in my mind that Maggie's behaviors that morning were defensive and protective. She wasn't going to let those other dogs get near me, and she knew I needed her warmth to protect me in the cold. Her instantaneous and "just right" responses to my crisis gave me the "healing moment" I needed.

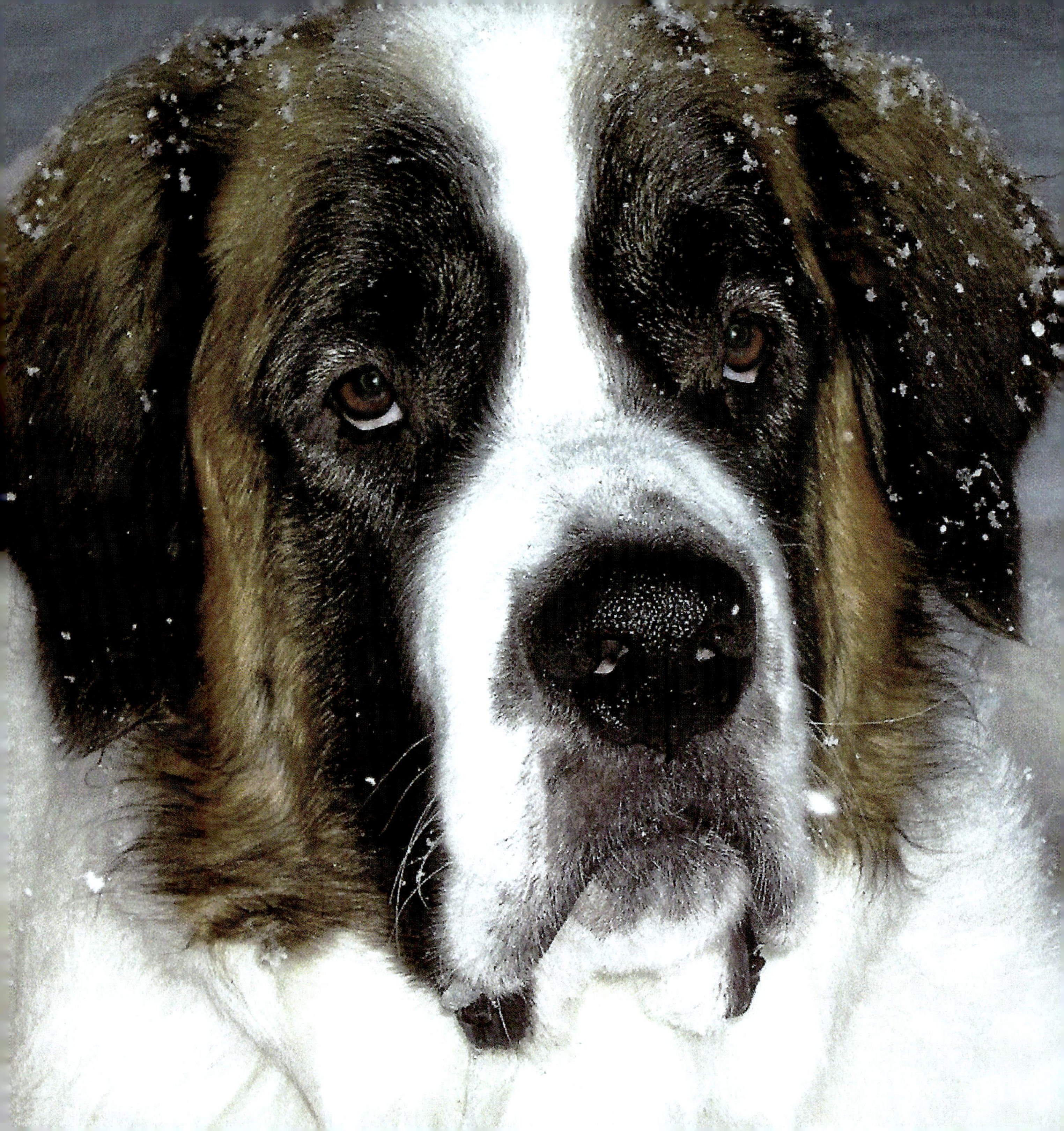

14
SUCCESSION PLANNING

I had a great problem on my hands. Patients and staff were frequently requesting visits. I had just accepted a new position requiring different work hours that lessened my availability for daytime visits with Maggie. So I began to think about adding another canine therapy team.

The hospital leadership team experienced a cycle of learning as we revised our policy and refined our process of selecting a new team. The policy identified the qualities of a pet therapy dog as mild mannered, having a calm and compassionate temperament, tolerant of stressful environments, elevator tolerant, and veterinarian health certified. Applicants had to have completed beginner and advanced obedience programs, canine good citizen certification, and pet therapy dog certification.

A selection committee was created to participate in team interviews. During interviews, the behaviors of the dog and handler were evaluated, mock scenarios were presented to the potential handler, and a bedside visit was simulated to observe the pet therapy team's interaction with a patient. The interview team was encouraged specifically to look beyond the breed of the dog and focus on the dog's actions demonstrated to the interview team members. Any size, breed, or mixed breed could make a wonderful therapy dog. For example, often rescue dogs make phenomenal bedside companions. The interview team was educated in evaluating the animal's natural ability and desire to connect and relate to humans other than the handler.

One lesson learned in the process was that patient perception is just as important as the temperament of the dog and the attitude of the handler. We had a young, very competent nurse on staff approach us about her Doberman joining our program. He was a 127-pound sleek, handsome male who had been through extensive training. During the interview, the dog was somewhat restless and yet very attentive to his owner. He tolerated everyone in the room but didn't seem to truly enjoy interacting with strangers. The interview team had concerns. Even though he appeared non-aggressive, would our perception match the perception of our patients if a Doberman came walking toward them in the hall? Would he provide comfort and a healing touch? We surveyed over thirty patients and determined that at least one-third of them found the description of him frightening and non-therapeutic. I was disappointed, as I knew his handler was just as passionate about her dog as I was mine. He just wasn't suited to play that role.

I have always thought God had His hand in every step of this journey, including finding the right individuals to assist Maggie and me in our pet therapy mission. I had considered approaching a close friend who partnered with an excellent therapy dog, but she was committed to serving the residents at a local long-term care facility. Just when I was feeling challenged by the difficulty of this next step, a gentleman named Dave approached me. He was retired, and had volunteered at the hospital for a while. He was kind, soft-spoken and respectful to patients and staff, had the time to devote to training a dog, and was very familiar with the organization's culture. He and I talked in great length about how he wanted to purchase a puppy that would be a great fit for therapy work.

Kandie offers a hug

He'd raised Saint Bernard dogs in the past, so he bought an adorable, pretty faced female named Kandie Kane.

Dave brought Kandie in periodically to share their progress as a potential pet therapy team. As the two worked together, I witnessed a healthy relationship mature between Dave and his dog that would be effective at the bedside. "The manner in which the volunteer communicates commands (to the dog) greatly influences how patients view the animals."[1]

After much effort, Kandie completed obedience class, canine good citizen certification, and therapy dog certification, as our policy requires. Like many other seasoned workers who are assigned to assist new staff members, Maggie was designated as Kandie's preceptor. Kandie consistently demonstrated her flawless temperament and ability to connect with patients. After about eighteen months, Kandie's lovely, calm demeanor and Dave's dedication earned them the approval to begin their work.

Dave had some great new ideas of where to offer pet therapy within the hospital setting. He and Kandie made regular trips to the chemotherapy room to visit with the oncology patients. He and Kandie also went to the outpatient infusion center, where outpatients stayed for a couple hours to receive their IV medications. I was touched each time I would see a crowd of staff and visitors gathered around to say hello to Dave and his gentle giant. They were quite an asset to our organization and would eventually receive an award through a therapy dog organization affiliate for completing three hundred patient visits. Little did I know that Kandie would soon fill a void due to Maggie's absence.

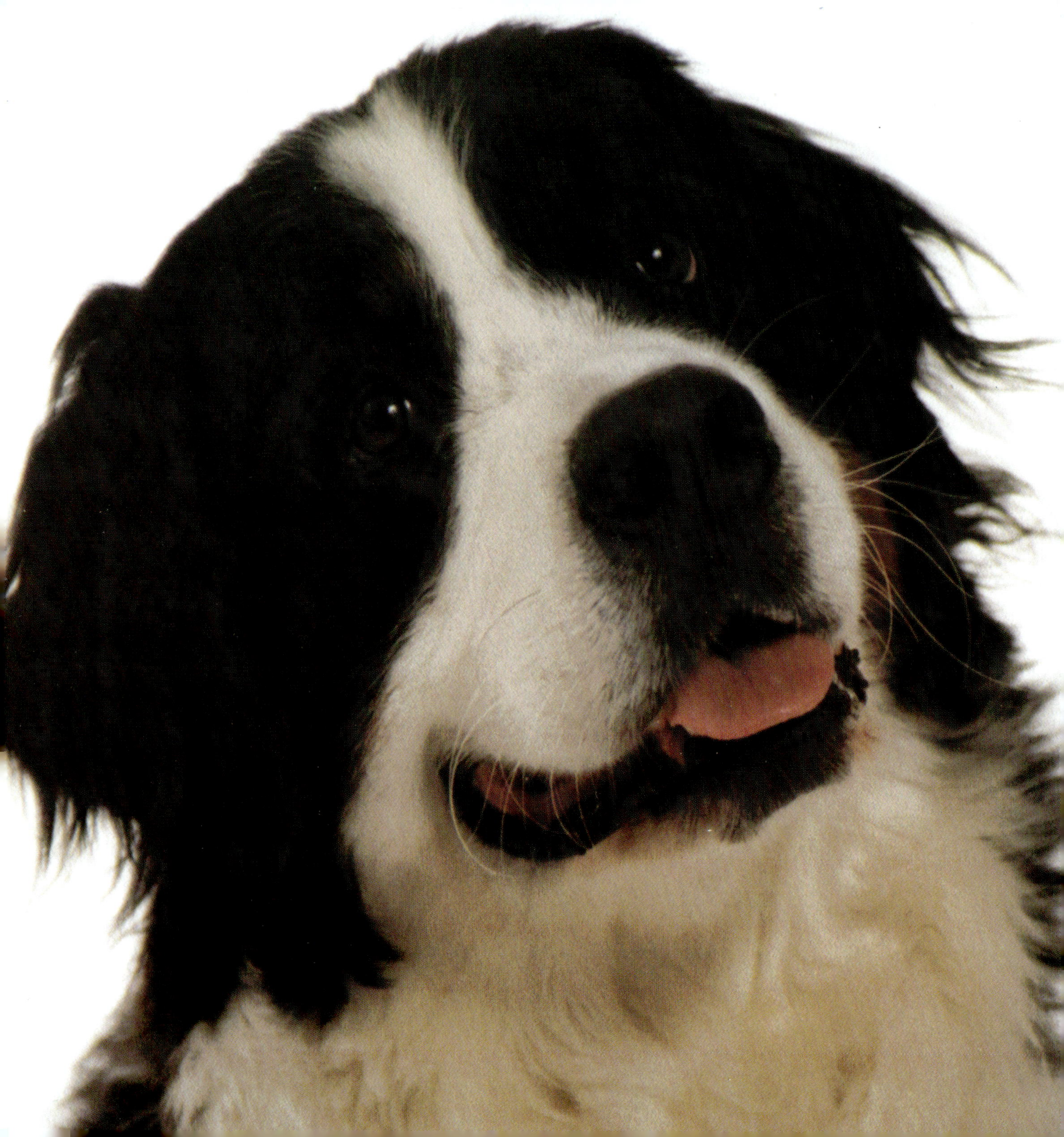

15
HER FINAL CURTAIN CALL

We had reason to look "extra spiffy" for our upcoming trip to the hospital the next day. Maggie and I had been granted an invitation to the hospital boardroom. Members of the administrative team were meeting with some Ohio executives representing a program on outstanding business performance. We'd heard that one of the guests was a huge fan of Bernese Mountain Dogs and owned two. We'd agreed that a quick welcome by Maggie would set a positive tone for the event. Just like many appointments in the boardroom, it was to be a well-planned and executed class act.

Our goal was a short and simple meet and greet. My research about the benefits humans experience with animals at their side had shown me that these four-legged creatures often facilitate rapport and interaction. Animals are able to set an upbeat tone and open a channel of safe, non-threatening communication between individuals in a group. They are great icebreakers and are often quite entertaining.[1]

Maggie was well-versed in her entertaining tricks, so all she needed was a good bath. As I rubbed shampoo all over her in my oversized mop sink, the nodules that protruded from below her rib cage reminded me of our vet appointment in a few days. I'd always been vigilant of Maggie's health needs. Several lesions had been biopsied, and the vet felt Maggie should have the four suspicious ones removed. It was a fleeting thought, and my mind went back to the rinsing cycle of her bath.

Maggie and I were the first to arrive in the boardroom. We positioned ourselves so we might see our guests entering. The bright light from the large window gave Maggie the appearance of being on stage and seemed to draw attention to her exquisite hair coat. Many of our patients over the years had marveled at her beauty, but this was my private moment. I found myself staring at her. I couldn't believe we had been working partners for over six magnificent years. She was aging, and I knew we wouldn't be together forever. I paused to seize the moment.

I had always believed that pretty is as pretty does, so I don't know why I was a little nervous. Maggie's demeanor was very predictable *and* pretty. The chief executive officer, chief financial officer, and vice president of clinical services soon arrived to welcome the guests from Ohio. When Mr. Paul, the apparent Bernese Mountain Dog fan, laid eyes on Maggie, his face lit up. I then introduced our greeter. "Maggie is here to welcome you to our hospital." Mr. Paul and Maggie shook hands, and upon my command, Maggie put her saddle shoe colored muzzle into her bag and retrieved a scrolled greeting. Mr. Paul and all others present expressed their gratitude for the "welcome to our hospital" message with refined applause, and then Maggie and I said our good-byes. We headed upstairs to begin our pet therapy rounds on the medical floors, I with a much more relaxed demeanor.

"Well, Maggie," I said to her on the elevator, "not many dogs have the privilege of going to the boardroom." She probably didn't understand that comment, but she stared at me and wagged her tail as I spoke to her. Unbeknownst to me, my fuzzy friend in her gorgeous fur coat had just completed her final curtain call.

The rest of the week flew by, and on Thursday evening my daughter and I discussed Maggie's vet appointment the next morning. I told Andrea, "I'm going to stay with Maggie while they remove those nodes, but it's going to upset me to see them cutting on her." Since I am a nurse, the actual procedure was not the problem. It was seeing my fuzzy partner lying on that table.

Andrea had always exhibited wisdom when it came to our animals' health concerns. She and I had raised horses for years and had lots of veterinarian contact. Those factors probably elevated her intuitive thinking. "Before you do that, I'd have them do an x-ray to make sure we're not dealing with a bigger problem," my daughter advised. That was a good idea. I would also ask Dr. Paul, the vet, about Maggie's new and intermittent dragging back toe.

Dr. Paul loved Maggie, and I like to think that perhaps the large portrait of her in his veterinary office lobby demonstrated his support for our therapy work. After I informed Dr. Paul and his respected partner, Dr. Lee, of Maggie dragging her back toe, the two veterinarians watched and listened intently as we made a couple trips up and down the hall. I shared with them the idea of having some radiology work done before the surgical procedure. They agreed with the plan. It didn't surprise me they would have to sedate her for the films, which they said would take several hours. I hugged her good-bye and went on to work, knowing there would be no surgical procedures done that day until after I'd heard the x-ray results from Dr. Paul.

Later that afternoon in my office, I was in a deep discussion with two of my colleagues when Dr. Paul called. He told me Maggie was still a little sleepy, but she had tolerated her sedation and radiology workup well. He then went on to say, "We did locate a mass in her abdominal cavity under her diaphragm." Asking the size of this growth, I recalled the nickel sized nodules on her belly that I had been watching.

"It's about the size of a dessert plate. Dr. Lee and I were able to palpate it while Maggie was asleep," said Dr. Paul. "The films also show some type of mass at the base of her spine, which could be causing her to drag her toe. We can discuss our options when you come to get her. Do you want me to proceed with the removal of those superficial lesions?"

I felt a lump in my throat and could hardly talk. "No, don't do anything else," I managed to choke out. "I'll be right there." I recall trying to make eye contact with my friends, but my vision was blurred with a steady stream of tears. Candy and Kim, both master degree prepared and experienced nurses, usually knew all the answers. They had nothing to offer concerning this shocking veterinary report but to listen.

Dr. Paul and I mulled over treatment choices. He felt the large mass in her abdomen might eventually create pressure on her diaphragm, which would impair her ability to breathe. He said he or the surgery team at Purdue University could surgically remove it, leaving an incision approximately 14 inches. If it did turn out to be cancer, he felt another way to manage her condition was chemotherapy. When he mentioned there was a good chance the lesions were cancerous, I recalled that cancer runs rampant in this breed. Although a seasoned nurse, I was not an expert in oncology. I did know, however, that Maggie was an anxious, prissy princess when it came to pain and when it involved being separated from me.

The car ride home with Maggie lying in the back seat was quiet. My mind was searching for a painless, non-invasive fix for this condition that had turned our world upside down. I lifted Maggie out of the car and created a sling using a beach towel to carry her hindquarters. She appeared very frustrated about this new immobility, so we were both looking forward to the sedation wearing off.

The next morning I had planned to call my close friend and breed expert, Lilian. She was also Maggie's breeder. I was searching for answers, but before I could make that call, I discovered more heart-breaking news. As a nurse I knew it only took a matter of hours for sedation to clear from one's body and to return to a pre-sedation state. So I was shocked and devastated to see that Maggie's ability to bear weight on her hindquarters was even worse than yesterday. She looked deep into my eyes for an explanation.

I called my daughter, the one who is so insightful when it comes to animal health. I explained that I'd have to be giving Lori, our animal caretaker while we're at work, special instructions on how to get Maggie in and out to potty. Andrea stopped me in my tracks when she said, "Why would you keep Maggie alive until Monday and make her endure all of this?"

I then put that call into Lilian and received a similar response. Although she lived over 1,000 miles from us, I'd kept Lilian informed of the tremendous impact Maggie was making with her pet therapy. Lilian listened as I tearfully relayed the news. A common phrase surfaced in my discussions with both Andrea and Lilian: quality of life.

"Janet, Maggie has taken care of so many people," said Lilian. "Now it's time for you to take care of her."

I don't recall much about the rest of that weekend except that Maggie and I, as my nieces would say, "hung out together." That Saturday evening as Maggie lay at my feet, I talked to her and composed a letter to her explaining the deep bond we had created during our very short journey of seven and one half years. We had developed an unconditional love between us that would last forever in my heart.

Sunday morning was beautiful. The sun was shining on Maggie and me as we sat on the front porch. She leaned against me, as was her habit, and we listened to the birds and watched the horses grazing peacefully in the pasture. The autumn leaves on the trees were falling, a gentle reminder that the season was coming to a close. How fitting. Then Maggie and I took our last walk down the drive, but this time I was totally supporting Maggie's hindquarters with a towel. We paused now and then to enjoy the simple pleasures of the day. Later in the afternoon, several friends came over to say their good-byes. As difficult as the idea of euthanizing Maggie sounded, they assured me it was the most humane option and best choice for my dog.

Five o'clock arrived all too fast, which was the time Dr. Paul had agreed to come to our house for the procedure. I sat out in the yard in one of Mag's favorite spots, and she lay in my lap with her head on my leg. With the sun shining on her beautiful, well-groomed coat, she looked like a perfect specimen of health. Dr. Paul, being quite a strong Christian, blessed this painful time with a heartfelt prayer. I held Maggie in my arms as he gently sedated her. She didn't question our actions, as she'd always trusted me to do anything with her.

Dr. Paul, his caring veterinarian technician, my husband, and our children all shared in this grieving moment. We each said our good-byes to my faithful partner one last time. Everyone present exhibited a touching tenderness as Maggie took her last breaths. She was buried with the letter from me placed by her heart.

THE VISIT

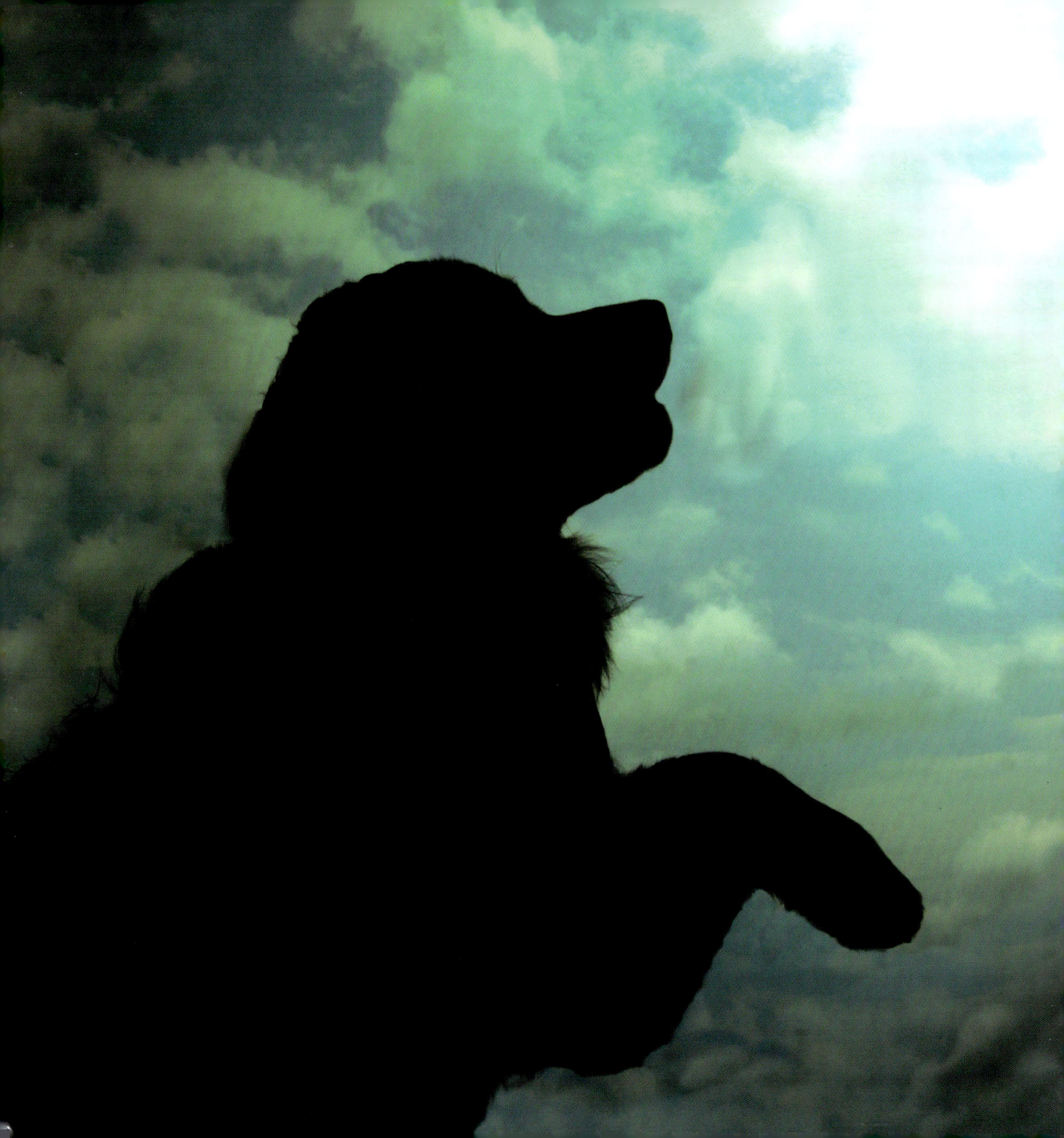

16
TRANSITIONS

Just plain empty was how I felt. I was one lost pup. The devastating event of saying good-bye to Maggie validated that she had been an integral part of my life. With children raised and out of the home, I had spent more time with Maggie than any other family member, including my husband. She accompanied me to the hospital, went with me to church sometimes, and was always by my side at home. Her role as a therapy dog had been closely intertwined with my professional life.

My boss at the time, the vice president of nursing, questioned why I came to work the morning after Maggie was gone. The answer was simple. I didn't want to stay home alone without her. At least I was at work with my peers, who seemed to understand. I did fine until I had to get on the elevator. When the elevator door closed, I had flashbacks of those memorable, private conversations Maggie and I had as we rode the elevator on the way to visit patients.

As I grieved, others grieved also. I received one hundred and fifty emails from fellow employees expressing their sympathy, as many staff members had grown close to her. Members of my family, my church, and those I worked with gave empathetic gestures in various forms. Two messages of sympathy were particularly meaningful. One physician commented, "You will definitely be in my family's thoughts as you grieve. The greater the love, the deeper the pain."

The minister of my church offered the other meaningful message. Here are his words.

> I will not forget that Maggie did the children's sermon when we first visited this church. That made a deep impression. When I was young, a friend wrote this song: 'All God's creatures have a place in the choir, some sing low, some sing higher, some sing out loud on a telephone wire, some just clap their hands, paws, anything they've got now.' This song reminds us that all God's creatures are cared for. Maggie's life and service have added praise of our awesome God, right alongside ours.

A close friend, Mary Lou, brought over some outdated Bernese Mountain Dog magazines. They seemed therapeutic for my grieving heart. In this stack of publications, I kept referring back to one photo of a large, majestic male named King Kohl. What caught my attention was his kind facial expression. I saw the gentle compassion in him that I had known in Maggie.

After Kohl had been on my mind for weeks, I finally called his owner to inquire if he was still producing puppies. She informed me that Kohl was almost ten years old and was no longer siring litters. She did refer me, however, to some of the owners of his offspring, who were known producers of litters. After weeks of phone conversations with breeders from coast to coast and emails from one breeder to another, I had to face the fact that none of them had puppies for sale. I also told myself I had to give up on the idea of owning a descendant of King Kohl.

During that frustrating time, I realized how rare and difficult it is to locate a quality puppy. Breeders are hesitant, understandably so, to place a top-notch puppy into a "non-show" home. I developed a respect for Bernese Mountain Dog breeders. They are focused on reproducing quality and are extremely particular about their litters' future homes.

One of my referrals was to Karen, a lovely lady and former ICU nurse from Michigan. She was a recipient of one of Kohl's offspring. As I shared my story and mission with her, she and I seemed to hit it off. Being in health care, she also knew the value of pet therapy. In the course of our conversation, she shared with me that her female had produced three adorable girls and one very laid back, husky boy. She said a common occurrence at her house was to find her male puppy missing from the litter box, as her daughter had chosen him as her snuggle partner on the sofa.

I was moved by Karen's story, and I melted when I received Bentley's five-week-old picture. What an adorable, chunky boy puppy with a most compassionate facial expression. The criteria I was looking for was a beautifully marked, very large male puppy with an outstanding personality. Unfortunately, Karen had shared that he was "sort of" spoken for to go into a show home. The decision would occur at seven weeks. But if Bentley didn't measure up to show quality, he could come live with me.

The weeks passed, and then the news came. Bentley, a grandson of Kohl, would soon become part of my family.

Bentley at five weeks

MAGGIE

17
STARTING OVER

After almost eight years with a well-trained dog who seemed to know exactly what I was saying and thinking, I was a bit shocked to return to the puppy stage. I can say, however, that from day one I was tremendously pleased with my new, big boy. Bentley was everything I had imagined. He was larger framed than Maggie, had a very kind way about him (like I'd imagined his grandfather had in those pictures), and had an absolutely phenomenal temperament. Not only was he beautifully marked, but he also had the "Swiss cross" white marking on his chest that typified the Swiss originated Bernese Mountain Dog.

Though anxious for a new pet therapy partner, I didn't want to overlook that fun puppy stage. I told myself to seize the moment and enjoy this adorable puppy God had given me. And I

A compassionate face at eight weeks

did. We had a wonderful first year getting to know each other, and I enjoyed introducing him to lots of people and new experiences. My family members grew to love him too. My son referred to him as the storybook dog named Clifford that wouldn't stop growing.

I was engulfed in raising Bentley and educating him in preparation for his new role when he received his first invitation to accompany me to the hospital. His presence was requested at a ceremony honoring Maggie's service. The hospital Volunteer Guild had donated a stately, granite stone with Maggie's headshot etched on it along with the text, "Maggie, Pioneer of Pet Therapy." It had been positioned in the front of the hospital next to a new spring flowering tree that had been planted in honor of Maggie.

On the day of the ceremony, many employees and hospital leaders, including our CEO and vice presidents, were present to recognize my former partner. My growing puppy and I stood beneath "Maggie's tree". The Director of Volunteer Services spoke many words of kindness related to Maggie and my dedication to our patients. As Maggie's proud handler and companion, I graciously accepted this memorial in her honor.

Unlike with Maggie, I knew when I first brought Bentley home that his upbringing would include a strong focus on preparation for pet therapy. With that focus in mind, I put some thought into how could we ramp up our efforts and raise the bar, so to speak. I recalled how much our patients had enjoyed Maggie's bedside

Julie teaching Bentley to punt a football

pet tricks. As Bentley finished the first and second courses of obedience training, his canine good citizen certification, and pet therapy certification, we were also learning some fun, new tricks. I researched several new ideas, keeping in mind what would work well at the bedside. He seemed to love performing and appeared amused by his own silly antics.

An outstanding expert, a dog trainer named Julie, gave me valuable help on how to teach Bentley his more difficult dog tricks. It was a "train the trainer" education. Julie made learning fun for Bentley, and she worked with both of us to accomplish some goals I didn't realize were possible. She taught me to focus on my dog's natural tendencies and strengths in considering what commands he could easily respond to. For instance, Bentley used his big, fluffy paws frequently, and I was able to teach him to "say hi" and put his paw over his face on command to demonstrate his "shy disposition."

Bentley started his job as a pet therapy dog in the fall of 2010 and seems to enjoy working with patients. He naturally becomes engaged with the patients' demeanor. He seems to understand when it might be appropriate to do some tricks and likes to show everyone what he knows. He has taken the liberty to begin demonstrating his repertoire of tricks without any cue from me, his partner. Because he is not quite a year and a half in age, he has a shorter attention span and tires easily. The length of time we are at the hospital is limited, and I assess him closely to see when he begins to tire and lose focus.

I hope to spend more time on some goal-directed therapy in which Bentley actively motivates his patients to achieve specific actions. For example, we worked with an eight-year-old who was challenged by the exercise of walking backwards. Bentley was entertaining as she controlled his leash and had him follow her walking backwards. When she gave him his back up cue of "beep, beep, beep," it was Bentley's turn to walk backwards. Seeing her expression was for me well worth taking some vacation time to spend in physical therapy.

An animal is often used to capture viewer attention in a way that a human cannot.[1] Bentley has been asked to participate in some staff education, and he is becoming a "poster child" for the hospital. Since he is a familiar face in the organization, his photo has already been included with some informative material for the staff. Bentley will be featured on the National Patient Safety Goals poster demonstrating the importance of checking patient armbands for proper patient identification. Also, he will be pictured in some fire safety education.

How ironic it is that Bentley, the pet therapy dog, will be used to enhance the hospital's safety projects. It was the Risk Management and Safety department that once challenged the expediency and validity of the hospital's pet therapy program when I first proposed it in 2002. Perhaps the change is due to the organization noticing the positive response employees have shown toward pet therapy and, most important, the therapeutic benefits to patients. And also, perhaps it is because the individual currently functioning as the Risk Manager and Safety Officer is this author!

Verifying patient identification

The Visit

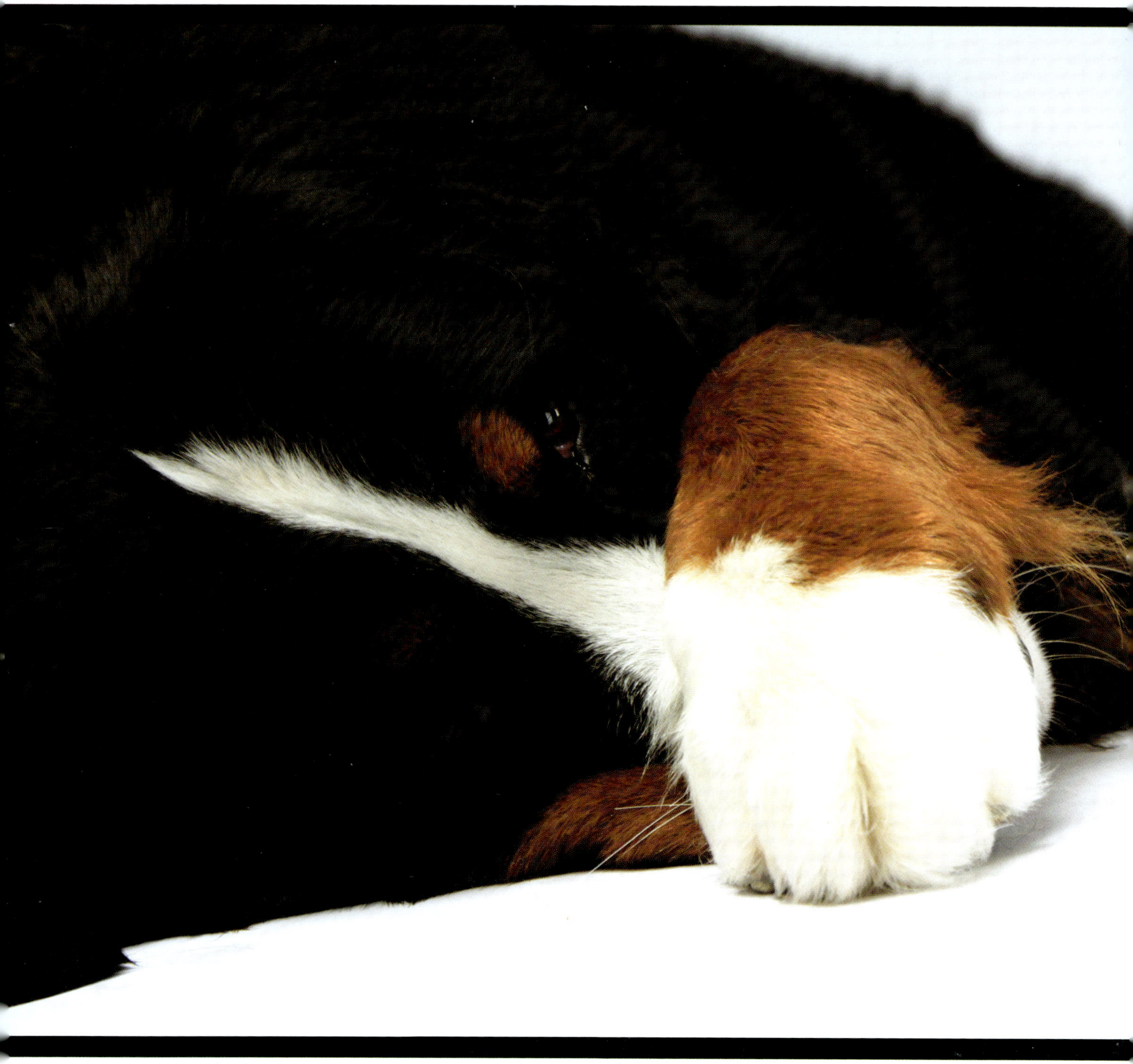

18
VERY BIG PAWS

It was a Saturday and the coldest day of the year, so I didn't take Bentley for our usual pre-pet therapy visit walk outside. That walk typically settled my young partner down before we greeted patients. Instead, I decided to briskly cruise around the interior halls of the hospital to remove all doubt that he might act a little too perky. I wanted him relaxed enough so that he could focus on his job, interacting with the patients.

The choice worked well and also turned out to be productive. At the end of our exercise, we met three physical therapists who were just finishing up their morning. They appeared as if they'd had a challenging day, but they seemed to be refreshed by the sight of us and interested to meet my new partner. One of the therapists said, "We've heard about him but had not run into him." I stepped inside their outpatient treatment room. So did Bentley as he maneuvered his way up to each of them as if to say, *"Hi, I'm Bentley. Nice to meet you."*

Bentley and I then quickly rehearsed his repertoire of tricks with our captive audience of physical therapists before we headed to the patient area. We did so each time we prepared for a visit, because Bentley was still relatively new at pet therapy. That day, as I prompted him, we demonstrated to the physical therapists what he had learned. "Bentley, are you excited to make lots of new friends around here? What do you think?" He responded correctly with his awkward little head nod. The therapists chuckled in chorus. After a few more tricks, Bentley thanked them for their warm welcome with his bow. The therapists commented that he, "the new kid on the block" therapy dog, had the potential to cheer up many patients.

I had observed my new partner closely as he studied each of the therapists, listened calmly to them, and gently wagged his tail in response to their comments directed to him. It was the first time I realized that perhaps Bentley had the potential to proudly carry on the legacy of Maggie. How could I be so fortunate to have the opportunity to accompany two effective therapy dogs? We headed upstairs to the inpatient area with this exciting thought in my mind.

Our first stop was in pediatrics. When the doors opened to the children's unit and Bentley heard the voices and giggles of little people, his ears perked up. We had barely arrived, yet Bentley found himself being taken for a walk by a five-year-old named Dylan. I stood and observed the two "youngsters" and was pleased that my 105-pound therapy dog was not the least bit intimidating to the children.

While Dylan and Bentley were entertaining each other, I stuck my head into another patient room where a three-year-old girl patient and her mother were lying in a hospital bed. "Would you like me to bring my big, fluffy dog in to your room and show you his tricks?" I inquired.

Dylan and Bentley—instant buddies

The smiling, outgoing little girl became quite animated. With her finger on her cheek, she pondered my question. "Well, I would really like for you to bring a kitty cat!"

That would be a difficult order to fill, since Bentley didn't know how to meow. But the little patient was soon mesmerized as Bentley answered his pretend telephone for her and handed her a box of tissues.

Our next goal for the day was to make some routine visits on the surgery floor where patients prepare and recover from surgery. I was pleased to follow one nurse's suggestion to visit a patient of hers. The patient seemed most grateful to interact with us but apprehensive at the same time, as the nurses were scurrying around to prepare her for surgery. We didn't plan to stay long, since I didn't want to impede the nurses' pre-op task list.

Bentley seemed to take a special liking to this patient. He climbed up in the chair next to her and stuck his neck out over her chest to look her right in the eye. She was a tall, larger framed woman. As Bentley's actions tickled her, she cackled a contagious laugh that seemed to shake her entire bed. She started making funny noises at Bentley, and he was mesmerized, cocking his head from side to side. Those two had her husband, the two nurses, and me laughing at their silliness. After about ten minutes, Bentley and I expressed our respect for their important schedule, wished them a successful surgery, and said our good-byes.

I've read about preoperative patients being under enormous emotional strains. "(In the preoperative patient) providing interaction with a therapy dog may help alleviate fears and promote a sense of well-being."[1] It certainly seemed to be true for this patient.

Passing by the nurses' station, I noticed it was about lunchtime. One of the nurse's family was there to join her for her meal break. Shannon, the nurse, asked if her daughter could meet Bentley.

The little girl, Meghan, was timid but definitely interested in being entertained. Shannon took a picture of Meghan and Bentley together just for fun.

Another nurse, this one from ICU, approached us. She asked, "Can Bentley come visit ICU Room Three? My patient is really missing her dog."

We headed down the hall in that direction. Room Three had four visitors standing around a kind, spirited, elderly lady resting in bed amidst multiple IV pumps and monitoring devices. When we asked her permission to visit, she sat straight up in her bed and said, "Absolutely!"

I am not sure whether Bentley climbed into her bedside chair without my coaxing because he thinks he's a human and that's where he belongs, or if he truly wanted to get up close and personal, but up he gently positioned himself right next to her. What really made a caring impression was when he clumsily reached his big white paw across her bedrail as if to shake her hand. She grinned from ear to ear and then suddenly apologized because she was without her dentures. Her family jokingly responded that Bentley didn't care about teeth. The patient was teary eyed when she rubbed Bentley's ears and said, "Oh, do I ever miss my baby." I'm pretty sure she was referring to her furry companion at home.

The patient's daughter mentioned that she remembered when my dog and I had paid a pet visit to her mom five years ago, and she vividly recalled the "tissue trick." I was amazed that she had recollected the details of that long ago visit. She then asked, "Isn't this your dog named Maggie?"

Bentley positions himself up close to interact with this patient

"No," I replied. "This is my new friend, Bentley." It warmed my heart that my former partner had left a lasting memory.

As we walked onto the elevator and the door closed behind us, Bentley looked up at me and let out a big, relaxing sigh. I gave him a pat of approval and said, "You're not Maggie, are you? You are handsome Bentley, and you'll do just fine. Everyone knows you have big shoes to fill, but then you have very big paws."

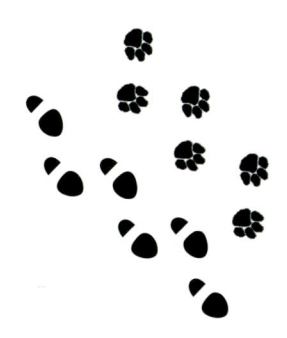

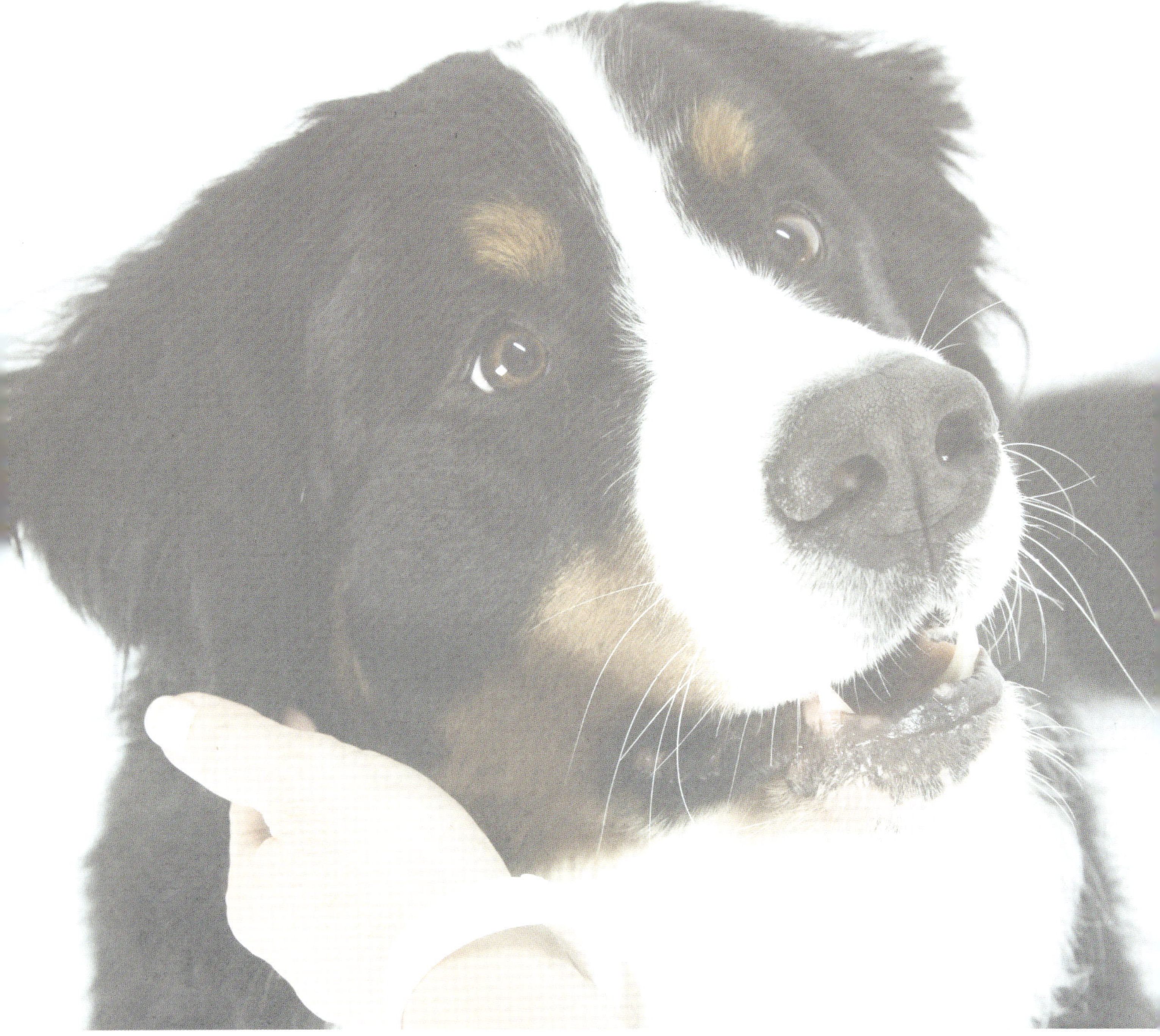

19
THE "HOW-TO" CHAPTER

Careful planning in all aspects of building a pet therapy program is essential. Nationally recognized organizations support the use of animals in health care. These associations are experts in pet therapy, have conducted research to support their guidelines, and are a tremendous resource in guiding the novice. Consideration of the following topics is necessary in building a safe and successful pet therapy program:

- ✓ Requirements of the pet therapy dog
- ✓ Characteristics of the handler
- ✓ Selection of a competent pet therapy team
- ✓ Health care setting preparation
- ✓ Pet therapy policy topics
- ✓ List of steps in becoming a therapy dog team

There is merit in using a certified therapy dog versus a family pet in the health care environment. Through the vigorous testing and health requirements needed for certification, these organizations are able to guarantee a healthy animal with the appropriate temperament and education. In some cases, these organizations also insure the dog during patient visits. Their required paperwork verifies good health and current immunizations.[1]

Characteristics of a dog under consideration for pet therapy are:

- ✓ Housebroken
- ✓ Tame and docile
- ✓ Clean—freshly bathed and well groomed
- ✓ No active disease or painful condition, blindness, or hearing loss
- ✓ Up-to-date vaccinations—follow guidelines of therapy dog association recommendations
- ✓ Calm, caring, compassionate temperament
- ✓ Relaxed when space is invaded, such as when bumped, jarred, approached unexpectedly
- ✓ Elevator tolerant
- ✓ Noise tolerant
- ✓ Eager to interact with patient
- ✓ Education level (obedience school graduate, certification as canine good citizen, and therapy dog association certification)

Characteristics of a pet therapy dog handler under consideration are:

- ✓ Understanding and strict adherence to patient confidentiality
- ✓ Comfortable around medical settings
- ✓ Pleasant, friendly demeanor
- ✓ Positive communication with therapy dog (versus harsh discipline)
- ✓ Respectful of needs of pet therapy dog
- ✓ Understanding of and adherence to infection control guidelines (example: isolation patient)
- ✓ Good communication skills and ability to interact with staff in order to gain understanding of patient needs
- ✓ Knowledge and compliance with hand-washing policy practiced by facility

A selection committee is a good way to evaluate potential pet therapy teams. This group would include the facility's key individuals and knowledge experts in the pet therapy process. An in-depth team interview can evaluate the therapy dog team using the following methods:

- ✓ Study the behaviors of the therapy dog team. Do they work together, do they give a positive image, do they exhibit behaviors that are focused on patient needs?
- ✓ Simulate a bedside visit that will paint a true picture of how the team will interact with a patient that the team has no prior relationship with.
- ✓ Give scenarios to the handler of events that could occur at the bedside to evaluate how the dog might react to real-life situations (example: patient suddenly does not feel well, patient acts confused during a visit, patient exhibits unstable physical or mental behavior, dog becomes restless)
- ✓ Accompany the handler and dog up and down some patient halls to evaluate the reaction by patients and visitors

There are many considerations for a health care facility, whether acute (hospital) or long-term (nursing home), including the following:

- ✓ Facility liability coverage
- ✓ Legal counsel
- ✓ Policy in place
- ✓ Department to manage the process and maintain current health/certification file on pet therapy team(s)
- ✓ Identified pathway of travel for teams entering and exiting the building
- ✓ Designation of areas that should not be visited (examples: surgery, recovery room, any isolation room)
- ✓ Designation of illnesses and diseases that would disqualify patients from receiving pet therapy (examples: immunosuppressed patients and those with pet dander allergies)
- ✓ Rule on whether the therapy team should sign in and out when on campus

- ✓ Dress code requirements for handler
- ✓ Badge requirements for dog (always wear badge or bandana showing certification)
- ✓ Process in place if animal would have an accident in the building
- ✓ Support and involvement of administration, physicians, nursing administration, infection control, risk management, volunteer coordinator

The pet therapy policy of the facility should be reviewed by all potential therapy dog handlers.

It should include the following:

- ✓ Description of the pet therapy team duties
- ✓ Dog requirements
- ✓ Handler requirements
- ✓ Selection process for hiring pet therapy teams
- ✓ Screening process for patient selection
- ✓ Designation of areas where pet therapy team can and cannot visit
- ✓ Health requirements of handler and dog
- ✓ Adherence to patient confidentiality
- ✓ Process that would occur if dog would have accident
- ✓ Pathway for pet therapy team to travel

There is an order to the process of becoming a therapy dog team. It includes the following:

- ✓ Select a dog with the appropriate temperament.
- ✓ Participate in obedience training.
- ✓ Expose the dog to multiple public places, learning to greet strangers.
- ✓ Continually access the dog as it progresses in training. Is it naturally friendly?
- ✓ Does it enjoy being around people? Does its behavior lend itself to pet therapy?
- ✓ Learn criteria for Canine Good Citizen and therapy dog certification.
- ✓ Become certified as a Canine Good Citizen through the American Kennel Club.
- ✓ Become certified through a reputable therapy dog organization.

Pet therapy can be an outstanding addition to any health care setting if offered in an organized and safe manner. Following the guidelines of the nationally recognized associations and preparing well prior to offering pet therapy are the keys to a successful program.

THE "HOW-TO" CHAPTER

ENDNOTES

CHAPTER 1
1. Connor, Katherine & Miller, Julie. (2000, July). Help From Our Animal Friends. *Nursing Management. Critical Care Edition,* (42-46), Retrieved September 12, 2002, from www.nursingmanagement.com

CHAPTER 2
1. Matuszek, Sarah. (2010). Animal Facilitated Therapy in Various Patient Populations. *Holistic Nursing Practice.* Vol. 24, (4): 187-203.
2. Biley, Francis C., & Brodie, Sarah J. (1998, May). An Exploration of the Potential Benefits of Pet-facilitated Therapy. *Journal of Clinical Nursing.* Vol. 8.
3. Hooker, Shirley D., Holbrook Freeman, Linda, & Stewart, Pamela. (2002, October). Pet Therapy Research: A Historical Review. *Holistic Nursing Practice.* Vol. 17, 1.
4. Federwisch, Ann. (2007, December 3). The Power of Pet Therapy. *Nursing Spectrum/Nurse Week.* www.nurse.com
5. Connor, Katherine & Miller, Julie. (2000, July). Help From Our Animal Friends. *Nursing Management. Critical Care Edition*, (42-46). Retrieved September 12, 2002, from www.nursingmanagement.com
6. Hooker, Shirley D., Holbrook Freeman, Linda & Stewart, Pamela. (October, 2002) Pet Therapy Research: A Historical Review. *Holistic Nursing Practice.* Vol. 17, 1.
7. Connor, Katherine & Miller, Julie. (2000, July). Help From Our Animal Friends. *Nursing Management. Critical Care Edition,* (42-46). Retrieved September 12, 2002, from

CHAPTER 3
1. McDowell, Betsy M. (2005, April/June). Nontraditional Therapies for PICU-Part 2. *Journal for Specialists in Pediatric Nursing,* Vol. 10,2.

CHAPTER 4
1. Dossey, Larry. (2007, July). Notes on the Journey: The Healing Power of Pets; A Look At Animal Assisted Therapy. *Alternative Therapies in Health & Medicine,* Vol. 3 Issue 4.
2. McDowell, Betsy M. (2005 April/June). Nontraditional Therapies for the PICU-Part 2. *Journal for Specialists in Pediatric Nursing,* Vol. 10, 2.

3. Heimlich, Kathryn. (2001, October/December). Animal-assisted therapy and the Severely Disabled Child: A Quantitative Study.
4. Heimlich, Kathryn. (2001, October/December). Animal-assisted therapy and the Severely Disabled Child: A Quantitative Study.
5. Dossey, Larry. (2007, July). Notes on the Journey: The Healing Power of Pets; A Look At Animal Assisted Therapy. *Alternative Therapies in Health & Medicine,* Vol. 3 Issue 4.

CHAPTER 5

1. Hooker, Shirley D., Holbrook Freeman, Linda & Stewart, Pamela. (October, 2002) Pet Therapy Research: A Historical Review. *Holistic Nursing Practice.* Vol. 17, 1.
2. Cole, Kathie & Gawlinski, Anna. (2000, February). Animal Assisted Therapy: The Human Animal Bond. *Advanced Practice in Acute & Critical Care.* Vol. 11 Issue 1, 139-149.
3. Swift, W. Bradford. (1997, March-April). The Healing Touch—Animal Assisted Therapy. *Animals.*

CHAPTER 6

1. Turner, Judith. Pet Therapy. *Gale Encyclopedia of Alternative Medicine.* Retrieved February 23, 2011 from http://www.healthline.com/galecontent/pet-therapy

CHAPTER 7

1. Federwisch, Anne. (2007, December 3). The Power of Pet Therapy. *Nursing Spectrum/ Nurse Week.* www.nurse.com
2. Mataszek, Sarah. (2010). Animal Facilitated Therapy in Various Patient Populations. *Holistic Nursing Practice.* Vol. 24, (4): 187-203.
3. Mataszek, Sarah. (2010). Animal Facilitated Therapy in Various Patient Populations. *Holistic Nursing Practice.* Vol. 24, (4): 187-203.
4. Heimlich, Kathryn. (2001, October/December). Animal-assisted therapy and the Severely Disabled Child: A Quantitative Study.
5. Heimlich, Kathryn. (2001, October/December). Animal-assisted therapy and the Severely Disabled Child: A Quantitative Study.
6. Dossey, Larry. (2007, July). Notes on the Journey: The Healing Power of Pets; A Look At Animal Assisted Therapy. *Alternative Therapies in Health & Medicine,* Vol. 3 Issue 4..
7. Biley, Francis C., & Brodie, Sarah J. (1998, May). An Exploration of the Potential Benefits of Pet-facilitated Therapy. *Journal of Clinical Nursing,* Vol. 8.

8. Eng, Brenda, Kassity, Nadine, & Sobo, Elisa J. (2006, March). Canine Visitation (Pet) Therapy Pilot Data on Decreases in Child Pain Perception. *Journal of Holistic Nursing.* Vol. 24, 1.
9. McCoy, Krisha. How Pet Therapy Can Help Autism. Retrieved April 3, 2011 from http://www.everydayhealth.com/autism/how-pet-therapy-can-help.aspx

CHAPTER 8
1. Mataszek, Sarah. (2010). Animal Facilitated Therapy in Various Patient Populations. *Holistic Nursing Practice.* Vol. 24, (4): 187-203.

CHAPTER 9
1. Life Application Bible: The Living Bible. Illinois: Tyndale, 1988.
2. Life Application Bible: The Living Bible. Illinois: Tyndale, 1988.
3. Life Application Bible: The Living Bible. Illinois: Tyndale, 1988.
4. Life Application Bible: The Living Bible. Illinois: Tyndale, 1988.
5. Dossey, Larry. (2007, July). Notes on the Journey: The Healing Power of Pets; A Look At Animal Assisted Therapy. *Alternative Therapies in Health & Medicine,* Vol. 3 Issue 4.

CHAPTER 10
1. Dossey, Larry. (2007, July). Notes on the Journey: The Healing Power of Pets; A Look At Animal Assisted Therapy. *Alternative Therapies in Health & Medicine,* Vol. 3 Issue 4.
2. Laun, Linda. (2003, January). Benefits of Pet Therapy in Dementia. *Home Healthcare Nurse. The Journal for the Home Care and Hospice Professional.* Vol. 21 (1): 49-52.
3. Laun, Linda. (2003, January). Benefits of Pet Therapy in Dementia. *Home Healthcare Nurse. The Journal for the Home Care and Hospice Professional.* Vol. 21 (1): 49-52.
4. Cole, Kathie, Gawlinski, Anna, Kotterman, Jenny, & Steers, Neil. (2007). Animal Assisted Therapy in Patients Hospitalized with Heart Failure. *American Journal Critical Care.* Vol. 16, 575-578.
5. Pet Therapy Holistic Online.com. The Benefits We Experience When Pets (Animals) Are Beside Us. Retrieved July 4, 2005 from http://www.holistic-online.com/stress/stress>pet-therapy-benefits-of-pet.html
6. Pet Therapy Holistic Online.com. The Benefits We Experience When Pets (Animals) Are Beside Us. Retrieved July 4, 2005 from http://www.holistic-online.com/stress/stress>pet-therapy-benefits-of-pet.html

7. Dossey, Larry. (2007, July). Notes on the Journey: The Healing Power of Pets; A Look At Animal Assisted Therapy. *Alternative Therapies in Health & Medicine,* Vol. 3 Issue 4.
8. Dossey, Larry. (2007, July). Notes on the Journey: The Healing Power of Pets; A Look At Animal Assisted Therapy. *Alternative Therapies in Health & Medicine,* Vol. 3 Issue 4.
9. Dossey, Larry. (2007, July). Notes on the Journey: The Healing Power of Pets; A Look At Animal Assisted Therapy. *Alternative Therapies in Health & Medicine,* Vol. 3 Issue 4.
10. DeCourcey, Mary, Keister, Kathy L., & Russell, Anne C. (2010, September/October). Animal Assisted Therapy: Evaluation and Implementation of Complementary Therapy to Improve the Psychological and Physiological Health of Critically Ill Patients. *Dimensions of Critical Care Nursing.* Vol. 29, (5), 211-214.
11. Biley, Francis C., & Brodie, Sarah J. (1998, May). An Exploration of the Potential Benefits of Pet-facilitated Therapy. *Journal of Clinical Nursing,* Vol. 8.
12. Intermountain Therapy Animals. Reading Education Assistance Dogs®. Retrieved April 2, 2011 from http://www.therapyanimals.org/R.E.A.D./html

CHAPTER 11

1. Biley, Francis C., & Brodie, Sarah J. (1998, May). An Exploration of the Potential Benefits of Pet-facilitated Therapy. *Journal of Clinical Nursing,* Vol. 8.
2. Roth, Joanne. (1999, December). Pet Therapy Uses with Geriatric Adults. *The International Journal of Psychosocial Rehabilitation,* Vol. 4.

CHAPTER 12

1. Bell, J., Bloniasz, E., & Giuliano, K. K. (June, 1999). Implementation of a Pet Visitation Program in Critical Care. *Critical Care Nurse.* Vol. 19 (3), 43-50.
2. McDowell, Betsy M. (2005, April/June). Nontraditional Therapies for the PICU-Part 2. *Journal for Specialists in Pediatric Nursing,* Vol. 10, 2.
3. Connor, Katherine & Miller, Julie. (2000, July). Help From Our Animal Friends. *Nursing Management. Critical Care Edition,* (42-46). Retrieved September 12, 2002, from www.nursingmanagement.com
4. Connor, Katherine & Miller, Julie. (2000, July). Help From Our Animal Friends. *Nursing Management. Critical Care Edition,* (42-46). Retrieved September 12, 2002, from www.nursingmanagement.com
5. Roth, Joanne. (1999, December). Pet Therapy Uses with Geriatric Adults. *The International Journal of Psychosocial Rehabilitation,* Vol. 4.

CHAPTER 13
1. Dossey, Larry. (2007, July). Notes on the Journey: The Healing Power of Pets; A Look At Animal Assisted Therapy. *Alternative Therapies in Health & Medicine,* Vol. 3 Issue 4.

CHAPTER 14
1. Connor, Katherine & Miller, Julie. (2000, July). Help From Our Animal Friends. *Nursing Management. Critical Care Edition,* (42-46). Retrieved September 12, 2002, from www.nursingmanagement.com

CHAPTER 15
1. Pet Therapy Holistic Online.com. The Benefits We Experience When Pets (Animals) Are Beside Us. Retrieved July 4, 2005 from http://www.holistic-online.com/stress/stress>pet-therapy-benefits-of-pet.htm

CHAPTER 17
1. Cstallion, X. (2011, February 25). The Use of Animals in Advertising. Retrieved March 26, 2011 from http://socyberty.com/issues/on-the-us-of-animals-in-advertising/socyberty

CHAPTER 18
1. Ingram, Lisa, & Miller, Julie. (2000, September). Peri-operative Nursing and Animal Assisted Therapy. *AORN Journal.*

THE "HOW-TO" CHAPTER
1. McDowell, Betsy M. (2005, April/June). Nontraditional Therapies for PICU-Part 2. *Journal for Specialists in Pediatric Nursing,* Vol. 10,2.

AFTERWORD

Animals have functioned as our companions and work assistants for centuries. To direct the capabilities of these two compassionate creatures, Maggie and Bentley, toward a broad spectrum of patient needs has been an incredible journey for me. In today's quickly advancing and high-tech medical setting, it has been especially rewarding for me, a nurse, to facilitate worthwhile and gratifying interactions between these therapy dogs and each individual they encountered. The healing relationship that Maggie and later Bentley created with all types of patients offered an additional, simple, yet very successful genre of care.

Many patients and staff have commented on the vast amount of knowledge I must have instilled in my furry partners. Actually, it didn't compare to the huge lessons they taught me about treating everyone with kindness, acting toward all individuals in the same manner despite their appearance or disabilities, and focusing on the needs of others.

Not all of our visits were earth-shattering events. Some were unassuming, simple diversions from the worries that accompany illness. My hope is that these heart-warming excerpts from my journey and the supporting evidence of positive outcomes will inspire others to partner up with their furry friends in this curative path. Perhaps other readers will be motivated to integrate pet therapy into the care plan of their loved ones who bear challenging health concerns. I also invite bedside nurses and physicians to consider pet therapy as an adjunct, holistic alternative for managing pain, anxiety, and stress in their patients.

Looking ahead, I can see many still untouched avenues to explore in terms of patient needs. I continue to search for best practices. What methods are other therapy teams using to most effectively connect with their patients to impact the patients' challenged world? Are these methods ones that honor and build on the utmost in importance foundation of pet therapy: the unexplainable and unparalleled connection that exists between animals and human subjects?

It takes time and dedication for a pet therapy team to address the spectrum of human needs, from medical to surgical patients and including but not limited to intensive care patients, pediatric patients, psych patients, demented patients, rehabilitation patients, and the elderly in nursing homes. I will be forever humbled by the opportunities I have been given and continue to be given to accompany my compassionate, four-legged therapists and companions on those VISITS, those HEALING MOMENTS IN PET THERAPY.

ABOUT THE AUTHOR

Janet Myers has been a deeply dedicated health care professional for more than three decades. Through years of patient care, nursing leadership, and now as Director of Risk and Safety, Janet has brought a rich diversity of health care knowledge and compassion to meeting patient needs. Her background, combined with her passion and work with dogs, has led to her mission of founding a successful pet therapy program.

As a pet therapy partner with her dogs for ten years in a variety of patient care settings, Janet developed a heightened awareness of the phenomenal outcomes of this complementary avenue of care. Her insights led her to create another pathway of therapy. In 2007, she and her four-legged friends began to do children's sermons, first in her own church and then later in several other churches.

Janet is a recognized speaker on the subject of pet therapy, its impact on patient care, and the data that supports the human-animal bond. She serves as a consultant to facilities desiring to establish pet therapy programs. To audiences large and small, she shares her heart-warming journey with her therapy dogs, Maggie and Bentley, to the bedsides of patients. Janet and her therapy dog partner work as a team in her speaking engagements, which have included presenting to the National Specialty for Bernese Mountain Dogs. Together they spread the message of the value of their work to dog lovers, health care providers, and families whose loved ones might benefit from this pace-setting program.

Her therapy dogs' ability to understand and meet the needs of the patients they "visit" is complemented by Myers' dog training capabilities. Janet has taken numerous dogs to obedience titles. By teaching her dogs an array of patient bedside dog tricks and applying them with her understanding of patient needs, she and her beloved furry companions have "raised the bar" in pet therapy.

Janet Myers resides in southern Indiana with her husband, Gary, her horse named Miss America, and her dog, Bentley.

www.thevisitbook.com
- to contact the author
- pet therapy program updates
- speaking engagements, book signings
- book information